Contemplatives
in Action

Contemplatives in Action

The Jesuit Way

William A. Barry, S.J.
and
Robert G. Doherty, S.J.

PAULIST PRESS
New York   Mahwah, N.J.

ROBERT J. WICKS
Spirituality Selection

Imprimi Potest
Very Reverend Robert J. Levens, S.J., Provincial Superior,
Society of Jesus of New England

Book design by Lynn Else and Theresa M. Sparacio

Cover design by Cynthia Dunne

We want to thank Robert E. Lindsay, S.J., James J. Martin, S.J., William J. O'Malley, S.J. and John W. Padberg, S.J. for carefully reading the manuscript and making valuable suggestions that have improved it. We are also grateful to Robert Wicks for suggesting the topic of Jesuit spirituality to us.

Library of Congress Cataloging-in-Publication Data

Barry, William A.
    Contemplatives in action : the Jesuit way / William A. Barry and Robert G. Doherty.
      p.   cm.
    Includes bibliographical references.
    ISBN 0-8091-4112-4
    1. Jesuits—Spiritual life. 2. Spirituality—Catholic Church. I. Doherty, Robert G.
II. Title.
BX3703 .B27 2002
255'.53—dc21

                                        2002005835

Published by Paulist Press
997 Macarthur Boulevard
Mahwah, New Jersey 07430

www.paulistpress.com

Printed and bound in the
United States of America

CONTENTS

To the Memory of Pedro Arrupe, S.J.

General Superior of the Society of Jesus
from 1965 to 1983

1. Introduction

ome years ago a student in his last year at a Jesuit university had the insight that he owed two of the most formative periods of his life to Ignatius of Loyola—his high school years at a Jesuit high school and his four years at this institution. If Ignatius had not been converted, or if he had died from the wounds he suffered in the battle at Pamplona, then these institutions that had so influenced him and so many others would not have existed. He felt deep gratitude to Ignatius, to the Jesuit order and to God. Countless men and women around the world over the past 460 years might have had the same insight. The Society of Jesus, founded by Ignatius and nine companions in 1540, has played a significant role in the life of individuals, of communities and of cultures. It continues to exert great influence. What is the source of its vitality? Why does it still evoke fierce loyalty and fierce opposition? We believe that its spirituality is the source of its continued vitality and also of the controversies that continue to swirl around it.

We write for a wide audience. There are over one million living alumni/ae of Jesuit high schools, colleges and universities in the United States alone. We hope that many of them may be interested in the spirituality that had an influence on their education. Many men and women who are not Jesuits collaborate with Jesuits in apostolic work: teachers, administrators, professional staff. Many of them want to know what makes Jesuits tick. Trustees of institutions with a Jesuit history have a responsibility not only to the state that grants incorporation, but also to the spirit that animated the foundation of the institution. This book, we hope, will help them to carry out this responsibility. Since Jesuit spirituality is a spirituality of Christian discipleship, the book may be of interest to all those who are called to Christian discipleship in the world. We hope that the book will benefit all who read it.

THE MEANING OF SPIRITUALITY

What is a "spirituality?" It is an elusive subject. At the least we can say that it refers to a person's or a group's response to God, that is, to the concrete ways that a person or a group relates to life's ultimate questions. A spirituality, therefore, refers first to the ways an individual or a group enact their religious spirit; only secondarily does it refer to a fully pondered upon and systematized set of characteristics of that particular enactment. A spirituality is, as the "Formula of the Institute of the Society of Jesus" puts it, "a pathway to God."

Since spirituality in this sense develops in historical people and not in the abstract, there are multiple spiritualities. For example, we speak of Christian, Hindu, or Buddhist spirituality, of Roman Catholic, Anglican or Methodist spirituality, of Benedictine, Franciscan, or Dominican spirituality, of nineteenth-century French or fifteenth-century Flemish spirituality, and of Ignatian spirituality. As soon as we speak in this fashion of different spiritualities, we realize that any spirituality is rooted in a particular historical and cultural setting. Indeed, just as culture is carried by a living tradition, so too is a particular spirituality.

Spirituality, even though culturally influenced, has a built-in safeguard against cultural encrustation; any spirituality defined as we have been suggesting posits the active presence of God in human affairs. Whereas our political, legal and scientific culture often seems to consider belief in divine intervention irrational, any spirituality worth its salt banks on such intervention. Such a spirituality expects that God is actively pursuing God's intention in the one action that is the universe, that, therefore, the Divine is continually trying to break through the encrustation of any specific culture to reveal God's own reality and desires. The trick is, of course, to develop ways of noticing those interventions, ways of letting the crust of culture be dented enough so that we pay attention. Indeed, one way to differentiate spiritualities might well be by the specific ways they try to help devotees to let God break through such encrustation. For example, Benedictine spirituality demands fidelity to the monastic order of prayer, work and hospitality with the assumption that such fidelity will allow God to be experienced in surprising ways. Jesuit spirituality, on the other hand, demands attention to the personal experiences that occur in the course of arduous, demanding ministry in the world to discover how God is acting in a person's life.

Any specific spirituality derives from an experience or series of experiences of God that a group has. Any such experience is never, of course, a pure experience of God. Every human experience is multidimensional. It is the product of an encounter between something and a person with a psychological, social and cultural history. Benedictine spirituality with its vow of stability was the product of an encounter between God and Benedict and his followers who grew up at the time of the breakup of the Roman Empire, when stable institutions were few and far between. Ignatian spirituality evolved from the encounter between God and a late medieval Basque noble and warrior at the time of the dissolution of the medieval synthesis. Methodist spirituality developed from the religious experience of John Wesley and his followers as they tried to cope with the effects of the Industrial Revolution in England. The point is that any spirituality is the product of an encounter between God and a group of human beings with a particular history that includes psychological, social, and cultural influences, among others.

The title of this book refers to Jesuit spirituality, not Ignatian spirituality. Jesuit spirituality can be considered a subset of Ignatian spirituality. Millions of people who are not members of the Society of Jesus, indeed many of whom are not Roman Catholics, have embraced Ignatian spirituality. Ignatius of Loyola composed the *Spiritual Exercises* as a handbook for helping all kinds of people to find God and to order their lives in accordance with the God they find. Based on his own experiences, he came to believe that God is actively at work in this world and wants all human beings to act in tune with God's intention. This is the heart of the spirituality of the *Exercises*. It is a spirituality open to all Christians and one that has helped millions in the over 450 years of its existence. One of Ignatius' closest collaborators, Jerónimo Nadal, believed that the *Exercises* could be adapted for use even with non-Christians. Jesuit spirituality, on the other hand, is the spirituality not of one man, but of a religious order in the Roman Catholic Church. It is expressed not only in the *Spiritual Exercises*, but also in the *Constitutions of the Society of Jesus* and in many other documents, and in the traditions and activities that have developed over the more than 450 years of the existence of the Society. Other religious congregations, especially congregations of women, have taken Jesuit spirituality as part of their own. It is the spirituality of the Society of Jesus that we will discuss in this little book.

We will endeavor to delineate those features of Jesuit spirituality that make it distinctive. In recent years it has been remarked that Jesuit spirituality is a spirituality of tensions. In *The First Jesuits*, John O'Malley, S.J. spells out some of the polarities that characterized the early Jesuits. They wanted to be peacemakers, but were often led into controversy. They were for reform of the church, by which they meant the institutional church, but adamantly strove to stay out of the hierarchy. They were doctrinally cautious, but often found themselves closer spiritually to those who got into trouble with the institutional church. They appreciated the rational scholastic theology of Thomas Aquinas, but wanted to be known for a theology of the heart. They had an organization that was built on the need for frank consultation and on trust in the enterprise of the members, but developed a vocabulary of obedience that seems to stress the autocratic rule of superiors. They were teachers of prayer, but saw the world, not the cloister, as their home. They had the cultural prejudices of their time with regard to women, but ministered to women in the same way as they ministered to men. They stressed fidelity to divine inspiration in the individual, yet defended the laws, institutions and customs of the hierarchical church and the religious community.

In the light of these polarities we can describe Jesuit spirituality by a set of life-giving and creative tensions. Jesuits are to be men of prayer for whom spiritual means are primary, yet they are asked to use all the natural means at their disposal for their apostolic work. They are to be disciplined men purified of inordinate attachment to worldly values, yet actively engaged in the world; they are, indeed, expected to find God in their activity. They are to be distinguished by their poverty, yet able to carry out their apostolic activities among the wealthy as well as among the poor. Jesuits are to be chaste and to be known as chaste, but are expected to be warm and loving companions at home and on the road, that is outside of cloister. They are to be men of passion, intelligence, initiative and creativity, yet responsive in obedience to superiors. They are to be committed to the people and institutions with which they are involved, yet able to move quickly to whatever place superiors send them. They are expected to be men who believe that God's Spirit communicates directly with individuals, including themselves, and thus who are discerning regarding the movements of their hearts, yet also to be men distinguished by disciplined obedience and fidelity to the institutional church. In the book of the *Spiritual Exercises* itself this tension is evident; the fifteenth "preliminary observation," with its premise that God communicates to individuals, sits in tension with the "Rules for Thinking with the Church" [352ff.].

Jesuit spirituality functions best when these tensions are alive and clearly felt, that is, when Jesuits experience in themselves the pulls of both sides of each polarity. Jesuits are at their best, for example, when they are attracted to spending much time in prayer and have to control that attraction for the sake of their apostolic activity, or when Jesuit theologians experience the tension of being faithful Roman Catholics and of searching for new ways to express the truths of faith in a different age and culture.

Because of these dynamic creative tensions Jesuit spirituality has been caricatured in the past and the present. Ignatius himself, for example, was accused of being influenced by the Spanish *alumbrados* (the "enlightened ones") of the fifteenth and sixteenth centuries because the *Spiritual Exercises* presumed that God communicates personally with individuals, and not just through the institutional church. In more recent times, Jesuit spirituality has been caricatured as rationalistic and coldly ascetical. Not only have outsiders caricatured Jesuit spirituality, but it has also appeared at times to be like these caricatures. In Ignatius' own time, some of the more prominent Jesuits of Portugal wanted to imitate monks who devoted long hours each day to solitary prayer, evoking from Ignatius strong reprimands. At times there have been Jesuits who became so immersed in the world that they

5

seemed to have lost their religious impetus and to be indistinguishable from their worldly counterparts. An example is Antoine Lavalette who, as superior of the Jesuits in Martinique, engaged in secret business transactions which eventually caused huge financial losses and lawsuits against the Society of Jesus in France, and which were the proximate occasion for the expulsion of the Jesuits from France in the eighteenth century. Prior to Lavalette's appointment as superior, the general superior was warned against him in these words: "...he will administer the Mission with human and political concerns; he is too self-confident and will undertake new ventures if he does not have a prudent superior to warn and rein him in."

As we shall see, Ignatius was aware of the dangers of the spirituality he and his early companions were developing, but he believed that God wanted this concrete Society with its spirituality. He tried to do his part through the *Constitutions*, through constant letter writing and through the tireless journeys of Jerónimo Nadal, sent to explain "our way of proceeding." Indeed, those words, "our way of proceeding," have become the Jesuits' way of speaking of their spirituality. We now turn to the founding of that spirituality.

2. "To Help Souls":
The Origins of Jesuit Spirituality

very spirituality develops in the minds and hearts of particular people as a response to the crisis of their age and culture. Ignatius of Loyola (1491–1556), baptized Iñigo, grew up in a Spain that was at the height of its powers. Ferdinand and Isabella had freed the last parts of Spain from Moorish hegemony around the time of his birth and, a year later, financed the voyages of Columbus that extended their rule to new lands and fueled an economic expansion that was staggering. At the same time he grew up as the medieval synthesis that had dominated European civilization was breaking up. Wars were incessant, and pitted small and large kingdoms against one another. Religious ferment roiled Europe, culminating in Luther's proclamation of the ninety-five theses at Wittenburg in 1517. In Spain the Inquisition vigorously pursued any semblance of heresy. Iñigo grew up in a climate where grand deeds not only were celebrated but also were called for, where issues of orthodoxy were argued and fought over.

Iñigo was born into a noble Basque family with a history of fierce loyalty to the kings of Castile. It was a family known for its bravery in battle and its propensity to violence. He showed himself a true son of such a family. He used the fact that his father had had him tonsured as a fledging cleric in order to escape a trial for some grave crimes committed at night and with full premeditation, and on another occasion he had to be restrained by his comrades from getting into a sword fight over a petty insult. On the other hand, he showed great bravery and loyalty when a superior force of French soldiers besieged Pamplona; indeed, the garrison surrendered only when Iñigo was badly wounded. During his recuperation from that wound he displayed his vanity, ambition

7

and courage again when he endured a second operation to mend his wounded leg so that he could make a fine appearance at court. Jesuit spirituality is rooted in the experiences of this brave, ambitious, swashbuckling romantic who lived in the tumultuous times that saw the beginning of the modern era of European civilization. His passionate heart still beats at the core of the spiritual vision that bears his name even to this day.

During his convalescence at the castle of the Loyolas, now ruled by his brother, Iñigo wanted to read some of the romances popular in his time, but the only books available were a life of Christ and a book of the lives of the saints. Ignatius began to read these. He also engaged in daydreams that occupied him for hours at a time. In one set of such daydreams he imagined the great deeds of chivalry he would do to win the favor of a great lady. After he had begun to do the spiritual reading, he began to engage in another set of daydreams in which he would do great deeds for Christ, doing even greater deeds than did the great saints. Both sets of daydreams gave him great pleasure while he was engaged in them, but after the first set he found himself "dry and discontented," while after the second set he remained "content and happy." He continues:

> But he wasn't investigating this, nor stopping to ponder this difference, until one time when his eyes were opened a little, and he began to marvel at this difference in kind and to reflect on it, picking it up from experience that from some thoughts he would be left sad and others happy, and little by little coming to know the difference in kind of spirits that were stirring: the one from the devil, the other from God. ("Reminiscences" in *Personal Writings*, p. 15)

From this small seed grew what eventually became Jesuit spirituality. Iñigo, for the first time, realized that God could stir his heart in order to draw him in one direction. In addition, he realized that God had an enemy who was also trying to draw his heart in a different and conflicting direction.

Iñigo now began a spiritual journey that led, after many detours, to the founding of the Society of Jesus. He spent almost a year in the small town of Manresa in Spain—by accident, it seems. Here he engaged in long hours of prayer. Here he learned who God really is in the hard struggle with scruples over the sins of his earlier life, a struggle that led him to thoughts of suicide. In the process he found little help from spiritual masters or from confessors. In the hard school of nearly a year's "novitiate," Iñigo learned how to discern the spirits that were agitating his heart. He came to realize that God is not a bloodhound sniffing out all his secret sins to torment him, but a loving Father who wants him as a companion to his Son. During these long months Iñigo fell in love with Jesus and his mission, and in the process discovered a way to help souls like himself who wanted to be one with the Lord in prayer and in work. He wrote down his insights, and these writings eventually developed into the handbook, *The Spiritual Exercises*, arguably the most important spiritual classic of the last 450 years.

Already we see some of the characteristics of Jesuit spirituality. Iñigo was close to being theologically and spiritually illiterate when he began his spiritual journey. He could, in himself, find no reason why God singled him out. He was neither learned nor particularly pious and holy. Thus, he came to believe that God was calling everyone to intimacy and to service. Jesuit spirituality has ever remained remarkably optimistic in its expectations of God's desire for closeness with everyone. In addition, he realized that God worked through events in his life, a realization that was the germ of another hallmark of Jesuit spirituality, the notion of finding God in all things. Iñigo found God by paying attention to what was going on in his mind and heart as a result of his reading and his daydreams. Eventually Ignatius, as Iñigo later began to call himself, developed a practice of examining himself often during the course of a day in order to find the hand of God in ordinary experience. Jesuit spirituality is distinguished from other spiritualities by this personal attention to feelings, desires, dreams, hopes and thoughts. In the history of spirituality this is known as a "kataphatic" type of spirituality, to distinguish it from an "apophatic" spirituality. The latter eschews subjective images, desires, dreams and aims to concentrate the person's attention on the repetition of a phrase or a short prayer and the self-emptying of one's concerns. Apophatic spirituality is exemplified in modern times by centering prayer and the type of meditation fostered by such monks as John Main, Lawrence Freeman and Basil Pennington.

On the basis of his own experience Ignatius came to believe that God and the devil, "the enemy of human nature," were engaged in a winner-take-all battle for the hearts and minds of everyone. He developed and codified two sets of rules for discerning the spirits, for testing what in one's experience is from God, and what is not. Discernment of spirits is one defining characteristic of Jesuit spirituality. Jesuit spirituality is centered on Jesus and his mission from the Father and his desire for followers who will continue his mission. It is oriented to service, to "the help of souls," as the early Jesuit documents liked to describe that service.

Finally, Jesuit spirituality is Trinitarian, based on Ignatius' own mystical experience of the three Persons of the Trinity and the active participation of the Triune God in our world. Ignatius, it seemed, experienced the words of Jesus as personally directed to him and to his companions: "'Peace be with you. As the Father has sent me, so I send you.' When he had said this, he breathed on them and said to them, 'Receive the Holy Spirit'" (John 20:21–22). Jesuit spirituality lives within the mystery of the Triune God working at all times to bring about God's intention for the world and calling men and women to collaborate with God.

During his stay at Manresa, Ignatius became absolutely convinced that God was calling him to spend his life after the manner of Jesus, helping souls in the Holy Land. He went to Jerusalem in company with other pilgrims, but, as he states in his "Reminiscences," determined "to remain in Jerusalem, forever visiting those holy places. And, as well as this matter of devotion, he also had the intention of helping souls," although he kept this latter idea to himself. When he spoke to the provincial of the Franciscans who had charge of the Holy Places about his desire to stay, he was told that he could not remain because other pilgrims who had remained had been captured and enslaved and had to be redeemed at great cost. Ignatius recalls:

> To this his reply was that he was very firm in his intention, and that in his judgement on no account should he refrain from putting it into practice; politely he made it clear that, although the Provincial

did not think it a good idea, he would not abandon his intention on account of any fear unless it was a matter obliging him under pain of sin. To this the Provincial said that they had authority from the Holy See to make anyone leave there or stay there whom they saw fit, and to be able to excommunicate anyone who was not willing to obey them. And in this case, it was their judgement that he mustn't remain.... ("Reminiscences" in *Personal Writings*, pp. 34-35)

We can see how strongly Ignatius believed that he was being led by God in his determination to remain in Jerusalem. But when he was threatened with excommunication, he concluded, "It was not the will of Our Lord that he should remain in these holy places" (*ibid.*, p. 35). Here we touch upon another hallmark of Jesuit spirituality: the conviction that authority in the church is also divinely willed. When authority's decision and one's own personal discernment come into collision and there is no way through the impasse, Jesuits will abide by the decision of authority.

After he returned to Spain from his pilgrimage to the Holy Land, Ignatius decided that he needed to study in order to be able to "help souls." People had begun to seek him out for spiritual counsel. In the course of his conversations with them he would explain his way of distinguishing mortal and venial sins. Authorities in the church began to question his credentials for speaking about such matters without any formal training in theology. Indeed, he ran afoul of the Inquisition on more than one occasion. He realized that he needed the credentials of sound philosophy and theology in order to continue to "help souls." Another hallmark of Jesuit spirituality begins to emerge: an insistence on intellectual competence and skill in order to "help souls."

In the years of his studies in Spain Ignatius began to attract followers who wanted to imitate his way of life. These early companions did not last. However, at the university in Paris he met young men of great ambition, intelligence and piety, among them Francis Xavier and Pierre Favre, his roommates. To six of these men he gave the *Spiritual Exercises* individually over a period of a month. Each of them came to the decision that he was called to follow Jesus in his mission of helping souls. When they spoke with one another after the completion of the *Exercises*, they were overjoyed to discover their common vocation. Like Ignatius they, too, would strive to go to the Holy Land to help souls. On August 15, 1534, Ignatius and these six companions vowed to follow Christ in poverty as priests and to go to Jerusalem to convert the infidels, on the completion of their studies. If they were prevented from going to Jerusalem, they promised to go to Rome to put themselves at the disposal of the pope. Before they embarked on the attempt to go to Jerusalem, three more companions were added to their number. These ten young men were the founders of the Society of Jesus, which came into existence with the approval of Pope Paul III on September 27, 1540. Another hallmark of Jesuit spirituality, then, is that it is based on companionship; it is a shared spirituality of service in the church.

These companions came from different countries and cultures. They found their common vocation by talking with one another about their experiences during the *Spiritual Exercises*. In Paris they would gather weekly to share a meal and spiritual conversation. They also helped one another in their studies. Through these shared experiences they became, in Ignatius' words, "friends in the Lord." When it became evident that warfare would not allow them to go to the Holy Land, they decided to put themselves at the disposal of the pope in Rome. The reason for the recourse to the pope was their desire to find God's will without being biased by their own nationalistic leanings. In Rome they confronted another question: Did God want them to form a corporate religious body or not? To answer this question they engaged in communal discernment for a number of weeks. They gave themselves to personal prayer and discussion of the question of whether they should form a religious congregation where they would vow poverty, chastity and obedience to one of their number. They spoke frankly and openly, discussing the pros and cons of each alternative. They decided that all would abide by the decision of the majority. In the end they came to the unanimous decision to ask the pope to approve them as a new religious order and elected Ignatius their general superior. Another hallmark of Jesuit spirituality is the frank, open and prayerful discussion of issues in order to find the will of God.

The decision of the first companions to put themselves at the disposal of the pope led to another characteristic of Jesuit spirituality: the desire to be more universally available for service in the vineyard of the Lord. This desire led them to decide to add to the usual three vows of religious orders a fourth vow of obedience to the pope with regard to missions. This vow has often been misunderstood by Jesuits and others, even to this day, and led to the characterization of the Society of Jesus as the "pope's army," a designation not much favored by most contemporary Jesuits because of its militaristic overtones.

Rather quickly the companions began to be dispersed around the world. Their initial self-image was of a band of men ready to move at a moment's notice to where the need was greatest. Where they founded stable residences in certain cities they were to live as beggars, having no stable revenue. They had decided that they could not even accept remuneration for any of their ministries. Often enough, as Jerónimo Nadal, one of Ignatius' key collaborators in explaining the *Constitutions* wrote, their house was to be the open road. This was a departure from the way religious life had been lived up to this time. Jesuits were not destined to live apart from the "world," but rather to find God in the "world," indeed in their apostolic activities in the world. They were not to give themselves to long hours of prayer, nor to the communal singing of the Divine Office as was the custom in all religious congregations. These departures from the usual not only caused controversy with church authorities, but also led to disagreements within the Society itself. Some of Ignatius' strongest letters were written to Jesuits, especially the Jesuits of Portugal, who wanted to engage in lengthy hours of daily prayer and in severe penitential practices. Indeed, he had to discipline one of the first companions, Simão Rodrigues, and remove him as provincial of Portugal because he was fostering both of these practices. (Simão also demonstrated another danger in Jesuit spirituality. His mission required that he be closely involved with the royal court of Portugal. Simão, it seems, became too attached to the court so that his obedience to Ignatius became somewhat slack.) The tension between the desire for union with God through prayer and the desire to serve the Lord in very active ministry led to difficulties early in the Society's history and has continued to be problematic since, as we shall see in a subsequent chapter.

The first Jesuits saw themselves as itinerant ministers of the word. As the number of companions rapidly increased, Ignatius found himself responding to requests for help from all parts of Europe. The request of the King of Portugal for some Jesuits to be sent to India led to the dispatch of Francis Xavier to that distant land in 1540, from which he then ventured to other parts of Asia including Japan. Many Jesuits soon followed him to these distant lands. By 1546 there were Jesuits in Brazil as well. Ignatius kept contact with his men in these far-flung territories through a letter-writing regime that is staggering, given the times and the difficulties of the mail. Ignatius wrote or dictated nearly 7,000 letters during his sixteen years as general superior. He did this while also composing the *Constitutions of the Society of Jesus* and administering a burgeoning new religious congregation, as well as nurturing a prayer life that was deeply mystical. He himself was a contemplative in action.

The request for help that had momentous consequences for the Society of Jesus came from the Viceroy of Sicily. He asked Ignatius to send some men to Sicily to open a school for boys, indicating that this would be the best way to evangelize the island. Ignatius decided to send ten men, some of the ablest he had at the time, to found the first "college" (equivalent to a modern-day high school) for lay students in the history of the Society. The success of this school led to requests for more such foundations from all over Europe, Asia and South America. Jesuits became schoolmasters and established a system of schools that is historically recognized as the order's unique contribution to the church and to culture generally. But with the establishment of schools the image of the Jesuits as a roving band of missionaries had to be modified. Schools required some stability of personnel and an attention to fundraising that changed how the Society operated. Jesuit spirituality was strongly influenced by this turn to the schools; from this time it became much more entwined with the intellectual culture of the world, with the powerful and affluent leaders of that culture and with institutions that required stability of personnel. Another tension was born. Jesuits now had to try to hold together a commitment to radical trust in God and in spiritual means, with an immersion in demanding studies and in the intellectual life of the age, along with the need to obtain endowments for their schools. We shall see how this tension played itself out in a subsequent chapter.

Ignatius and the early Jesuits found that they had to hold together in tension theology and spirituality. Theology and spirituality had experienced a disastrous divorce during the twelfth and thirteenth centuries. In the Spain of Ignatius' time this divorce showed itself in the struggle between theologians (and the Inquisition) and the so-called *Alumbrados,* the enlightened ones. Ignatius' *Spiritual Exercises* came under attack from some theologians, notably the Spanish Dominicans Cano and Pedroche, as being tainted with the heretical notions of the *Alumbrados* and of the Lutherans, because of Ignatius' insistence that during the making of the Exercises the director should not try to influence the directee toward religious life, but rather should "leave the Creator to work directly with the creature" (no. 15). At the same time as the Jesuits defended the *Spiritual Exercises* against such attacks, they advocated serious study of theology. John O'Malley puts the matter thus: "The Jesuits wanted, however, to provide that theology with a new casing and to direct it more effectively to ministry. Nadal expressed their ideal succinctly: 'to join speculation with devotion and with spiritual understanding...This is our desire. This is the underlying premise of the plan of studies in the Society'" (*The First Jesuits,* p. 244). In other words, Jesuit theology wants to arise from the experience of God and lead to a deeper experience.

Finally, we need to remark on a tension that runs through all the others, the tension in Ignatius and his companions between wholehearted commitment to concrete action in this world and openness to new initiatives from God. This tension can be seen in the way Ignatius gave himself to the pilgrimage to Jerusalem and to his resolve to remain in Jerusalem, as well as his willingness to give up this resolve when faced with the command of a superior who could order him under pain of excommunication. It can also be seen in the way Ignatius reacted to the question of how long it would take him to reconcile himself to the dissolution of the Society of Jesus, a not unlikely possibility in the first years of its existence. Ignatius said that he believed that he could be reconciled to this loss of his life's work in fifteen minutes of prayer. We will need to say more about this tension when we try to understand the Ignatian notion of "indifference."

The tensions in Jesuit spirituality came near to destroying or at least crippling it immediately after the death of Ignatius. Nicolá Bobadilla, one of the first ten companions, who had often chafed under Ignatius' authority, had the ear of Pope Paul IV, himself very ambivalent about Ignatius and the Society. The First General Congregation of the Society, held in 1558 to elect a new general superior, was clouded by the suspicions aroused in the pope in part by Bobadilla. (The highest superior of the Jesuits is called the general superior, as distinct from a provincial superior or a local superior. Unfortunately, by abbreviating the title to "the general," Jesuits have unwittingly nurtured the mistaken impression that the order is constructed like an army. Throughout the book we will use the full title "general superior.") Paul IV ordered the Jesuits to return to the monastic custom of singing the Divine Office at regular times during each day and forbade the newly-elected general superior, Diego Laínez, another of the first ten companions, to take the position for longer than three years. This was in order to prevent the "autocratic" kind of rule that supposedly characterized Ignatius' term as general superior. The Jesuits themselves, at the Congregation, were divided on some of these issues. Simão Rodrigues sided at first with Bobadilla. Eventually, however, the crisis was resolved. But we can see that the spirituality of the Society can lead even good men into strong disagreements. Not surprisingly, such disagreements have continued to trouble the Society in the intervening years.

In our own day the tensions of Jesuit spirituality have caused deep disagreements among Jesuits. There are, for example, Jesuits who believe that Pedro Arrupe, the general superior who led the Society through the years from the Second Vatican Council until his retirement in 1983, was one of the great generals of all time; other Jesuits consider him the symbol, if not the prime mover, of the loss of all that they had known and loved in their Jesuit lives—with the changes initiated by the Second Vatican Council and the Society's General Congregations 31 and 32. We shall have more to say about Fr. Arrupe in a later chapter but again, it is clear that even in our day good Jesuits can have strong disagreements. It lies close to hand to demonize one or other of the sides in such controversies, but often the controversy arises because the antagonists are unaware that the tension runs through the hearts of the men on both sides of the argument. Yet the tension can be a source of life-giving creativity.

3. "In Him Alone": The Tension between Trust in God and the Use of One's Talents

gnatius opens Part X of the *Constitutions* with these words:

> The Society was not instituted by human means; and it is not through them that it can be preserved and increased, but through the grace of the omnipotent hand of Christ our God and Lord. Therefore in him alone must be placed the hope that he will preserve and carry forward what he deigned to begin for his service and praise and for the aid of souls. In conformity with this hope, the first and most appropriate means will be the prayers and Masses which ought to be offered for this holy intention, and which should be ordered for this purpose every week, month, and year in all places where the Society resides. [812]

He then goes on to write about the means that unite the Jesuit with God, such as "goodness and virtue, and especially charity, and a pure intention of the divine service, and familiarity with God our Lord in spiritual exercises of devotion, and sincere zeal for souls for the sake of the glory of the one who created and redeemed them and not for any other benefit" [813].

Jesuit spirituality, like any Christian spirituality, begins with trust in God. But it does not end there. Ignatius continues:

> When based upon this foundation, the natural means which equip the human instrument of God our Lord to deal with his fellow human beings will all help toward the preservation and growth of this whole body, provided they are acquired and exercised for the divine service alone; employed, indeed, not so that we may put our confidence in them, but so that we may cooperate with the divine

grace according to the arrangement of the sovereign providence of God our Lord. For he desires to be glorified both through the natural means, which he gives as Creator, and through the supernatural means, which he gives as the Author of grace. Therefore the human or acquired means ought to be sought with diligence, especially well-grounded and solid learning, and a method of proposing it to the people by means of sermons, lectures, and the art of dealing and conversing with others. [814]

These carefully written paragraphs illustrate how aware Ignatius was of the tensions involved in the spirituality of this new religious order. He underlines the necessity of attention to the spiritual means because he is so cognizant of the dangers of honing the natural skills of the talented and ambitious men who were attracted to the Society. In this chapter we want to explore the tension inherent in the kind of religious congregation Ignatius and his first companions envisaged.

Ignatius, we have seen, was given extraordinary mystical insights during his stay at Manresa, insights that he himself acknowledged as surpassing all that he had learned in his subsequent life. He wanted to share what he had learned about God and God's ways with others. Yet he also soon discovered that he needed to study in order to be able to help souls. After some aborted attempts in Spain, he went to Paris to study at its university. There he realized that the methods of study in vogue in Paris were far superior and more orderly than those he had been exposed to in Spain. Ever after he extolled the Parisian methods of study. Thus, in himself he experienced the tension between infused mystical knowledge about the things of God, which he wanted to share with others, and the need for extended study in an orderly way in order to help souls. He must have been sorely tried when the various investigations of the Inquisition in Spain invariably found no error in his teachings, yet prohibited him from speaking of certain topics of morality until he had studied theology. God had blessed him with these extraordinary insights, not just for himself, but also for the benefit of others, but the authorities of the church would not allow him to use these gifts without study. Ignatius learned from his experience to trust in

God, but also to use all the appropriate natural means to get the message of God across. But primacy always had to be given to trust in God.

It is not easy to keep that primacy before one's eyes, especially if one has spent a great deal of time and effort in honing skills and imbibing knowledge. It might be easier to forego study and training in order to put all one's trust in God. One might say: "If I avoid study and training, then I will not be tempted to take pride in my own accomplishments." That is the temptation of the *Alumbrados,* the enlightened ones throughout the ages. The trouble is that this stance all too easily leads to stubborn insistence on one's "mystical gifts." This is one of the shoals that Jesuit spirituality has to avoid. Teresa of Avila, who came to appreciate Jesuit confessors, once remarked that if she had to choose between a learned confessor and a holy one, she would choose the learned one, a remark occasioned, no doubt, by the amount of bad advice given by unlearned confessors; of course, she also hoped that she would find a confessor who combined both.

It is more likely that Ignatius had in mind the other shoal as the more dangerous for the Jesuit, the shoal of reliance on one's talents and training. This seems the clear inference from the sections of the *Constitutions* cited earlier in this chapter. Indeed, throughout their history Jesuits have had to be on guard against this danger. If a man has spent years learning a discipline and the skills of teaching, it lies all too close to hand to trust one's knowledge and skills and to rely on them rather than on God. Not that he does not need to use all these skills and all the knowledge gained, but the danger is that use of these talents will become reliance on them. Inordinate pride in one's own accomplishments follows. How does one manage to reach a balance?

Ignatius believed that Jesuits needed a long, intense period of training in order to attain the balance. Moreover, this training needed to be practical, not just theoretical. The Jesuit novitiate consists essentially of "experiments," experiences that test the mettle of the aspiring Jesuit. The first of these is the making of the full *Spiritual Exercises* over a period of thirty days. These Exercises put the novice into the crucible of solitude where he is forced to face his alleged trust in God. He will confront his own self-will and sinfulness, his own fears and anxieties, his own weaknesses and strengths during days when he has few, if any, outlets that will divert him from this self-confrontation before God. His only conversation, aside from his conversations with God, occur in his daily meetings with his director. The director, however, has been trained to keep out of the way and to "leave the Creator to work directly with the creature" (*Exercises,* n. 15). During these Exercises it is expected that the novice will experience various movements of the heart that will agitate him and challenge him. He must learn to discern which of these movements are from God and which are not, and to put his trust in his discernment. Indeed, he must learn that faith in God means trusting in his discernments and acting on them. This "experiment," making the full *Spiritual Exercises,* is the heart of the novitiate experience for the novice.

However, it does not stand alone. Ignatius believed that the novice needed to be exercised in trust in God in various ways. One of the most severe such tests was the hospital experiment. The novice spent one month working in a hospital as an orderly. In Ignatius' time hospitals were dangerous places. Sanitation and hygiene were almost nonexistent; plagues were a regular feature of the cities and towns; and hospitals were places to avoid if one wanted to avoid the plague. But Ignatius mentions this experiment right after the *Spiritual Exercises.* Many novices never came back from this experiment, either because they died or because they could not take it and so left.

The third experiment is a month of pilgrimage without any money. The novice was expected to go from one point to another in the course of that month begging his way. In this way, Ignatius writes, the novice will "grow accustomed to discomfort in food and lodging. Thus too the candidate, through abandoning all the reliance which he could have in money or other created things, may with genuine faith and intense love place his reliance entirely in his Creator and Lord" [*Constitutions,* n. 67]. In the novitiate itself they will exercise themselves "in various low and humble offices," in teaching catechism to children, and other ministries. The Jesuit novitiate was not supposed to be a place for the faint-hearted and pusillanimous, not a "retreat" from the rigors of life in order to learn how to pray and obey, but a rather fierce testing ground to make sure that the novice had the goods to be able to grow into the kind of Jesuit who could manage the tensions of Jesuit spirituality.

Only after the completion of two years of such a regimen did a young man begin to do the studies that would make him an apt instrument for ministry. These studies were to consume most of his energies over a rather lengthy period of time. Ignatius knew from experience that such a long period of study could diminish one's trust in God and dry the ardor of one's heart. So he designed a third "probation," another period like the novitiate that he called the "school of the heart." In Jesuit parlance the first probation is a period called "postulancy" before novitiate, the second is the novitiate itself, and the third is this period after studies. Because it is third, this period is called "tertianship." During this period the Jesuit who has finished his studies, once again makes the *Spiritual Exercises* for thirty days and engages in some of the same experiments as in the novitiate. In the *Constitutions* Ignatius writes that

> ...it will be helpful for those who had been sent to studies, upon finishing the work and effort of intellectual formation, to apply themselves during the period of final probation to the school of the heart, exercising themselves in spiritual and corporal pursuits which can engender in them greater humility, abnegation of all sensual love and will and judgment of their own, and also greater knowledge and love of God our Lord; so that when they themselves have made progress they can better help others to progress for the glory of God our Lord. [516]

When the young Jesuit has finished this period, he is ready to be called to final vows by the general superior. It is hoped that he has had enough experience of the tensions of Jesuit spirituality that he can put all his trust in God as he engages in apostolic activity and yet use all his gifts and talents without anxiety and with abandon.

"Pray as if everything depended on God; work as if everything depended on yourself." This aphorism is often cited as typically Ignatian. However, it appears nowhere in his writings. In a collection of sayings attributed to Ignatius there is one that could have given rise to this aphorism, but its meaning is just the opposite. It can be loosely translated: "Pray as if everything depended on you; work as if everything depended on God." This translation fits the dynamic spirituality of Ignatius much better than the more popular one. According to Ignatian spirituality we pray because what we will do is important; our actions can be in tune with God's intention or not. We want to make sure that our actions are in tune with God's project; we want to get it right, in other words. So we pray for God's light and guidance as we ponder what to do. After we have discerned how to act in tune with God, then we can engage in that action with complete trust in God to bring about what God wants to effect. Thus, Ignatius spent many hours in prayer asking for divine confirmation of his decision about the kind of poverty the Society of Jesus should have. He wanted to get it right. Ignatius believed that it was crucially important for the health of this new order that God wanted it to exist for service in the church. But once he had decided and began to act on his discernment, he could leave the success of the enterprise to God. Thus he could say that if the Society were suppressed, he would need only fifteen minutes to be at peace.

The tension involved in trusting in God and in one's talents and insights can only be creative and live-giving if the two trusts are actually present in a person. It is, however, easy to let one of the trusts fade into the background. For example, it would not be in accord with Ignatian spirituality to put one's trust in God to such an extent in preparing a homily that one refused to read any commentary on the scripture texts of the day. When Ignatius began to study, for example, he found himself distracted from learning by great consolations. He decided that these consolations were a temptation because they kept him from doing the studies that would enable him to help souls better. It is far more likely, however, that a Jesuit will be tempted in the other direction, to put too much trust in his own efforts and planning. This temptation has led to a kind of corporate pride in the accomplishments of the order that seems to give only lip service to trust in God. One example will suffice. Just before Pope Clement XIV suppressed the Society, a Jesuit of great repute gave an exhortation to the Jesuit

23

community in Rome. The whole talk was devoted to blatant praise of the Society. The general superior, Lorenzo Ricci, ordered him to bring the text to him and, in his presence, tore it up and excoriated the man for his corporate pride.

Another Ricci, Matteo (1552–1610), the renowned "apostle of China," is an example of a Jesuit who was able to hold in tension great trust in God and the use of his talents. He was a skilled mathematician and a genius at learning languages. He had hoped to convert the Chinese people through persuasion rather than coercion. He produced some twenty books during his years in China, some of them still recognized as classics of Chinese science and literature. Yet his Jesuit companions all attested to his humility and holiness, and at Vatican II the Chinese bishops in attendance unanimously petitioned the pope to introduce his cause for beatification.

The correct understanding of the saying attributed to Ignatius gives us a glimpse into how the tension involved in trust in God and trust in one's own talents can be creative and life-giving. But it requires, as Ignatius wrote in the *Constitutions*, that Jesuits make every effort to "unite the human instrument with God" [813]. This leads us to the next chapter where we want to look at the tension of prayer and action that is at the heart of Ignatian and Jesuit spirituality.

4. "Fruitful Labor":
The Tension between Prayer and Action

n the *Constitutions* Ignatius prescribed very little formal prayer for the formed Jesuit, that is, the Jesuit who has pronounced his final vows after "tertianship." He writes:

> Given the length of time and approbation of their life which are required before admission into the Society among the professed...,
> it is presupposed that those so admitted will be men who are spiritual and sufficiently advanced that they will run in the path of Christ our Lord to the extent that their bodily strength and the exterior occupations undertaken through charity and obedience allow. Therefore, in what pertains to prayer, meditation, and study, and also in regard to the bodily practices of fasts, vigils, and other austerities or penances, it does not seem proper to give them any other rule than that which discreet charity dictates to them, provided that the confessor always be informed and also, when a doubt about advisability arises, the superior. Only this will be said in general: On the one hand, they should take care that the excessive use of these practices not weaken their bodily strength and or take up so much time that they are rendered incapable of helping the neighbor spiritually according to our Institute; on the other hand, they should be vigilant that these practices not be relaxed to such an extent that the spirit grows cold and the human and lower passions grow warm. [582]

Ignatius presupposes that the formed Jesuit will have strong desires for union with God in prayer and for penances. In this prescription he aims to temper these desires so that the formed Jesuit is not prevented from working in the vineyard of the Lord. He also mentions the opposite tendency, but it seems almost an afterthought. His main point is to make clear that the formed Jesuit needs to be discerning about the practices of prayer and asceticism

25

in order to be an effective apostle. Indeed, the formed Jesuit is supposed to find God in all things, especially in his apostolic activity. In order to understand Jesuit spirituality we need to make sense of this lack of precision regarding the amount of prayer to be practiced by the individual and the community.

Ignatius' prescription, or lack of prescription, regarding prayer was controversial in his lifetime and afterward. We have already noted the controversy with Simão Rodrigues and some Portuguese and Spanish Jesuits who wanted to engage in extensive daily prayer and excessive, even bizarre, penances. St. Francis Borja, the Spanish nobleman who entered the Jesuits after the death of his wife, had difficulties with the lack of precision regarding the amount of daily prayer and penance prescribed for a formed Jesuit. In letters to him Ignatius had to counsel moderation. Pope Paul IV exclaimed in an interview with the second general superior, Diego Laínez, "Woe betide you, if you do not pray! Cursed be the study, for which the divine office is omitted." When Borja became the third general superior in 1565, he asked that the General Congregation prescribe an hour of daily prayer in addition to daily Mass and two periods of examination of conscience. This became the norm for all Jesuits until the Thirty-first General Congregation in 1965–66 reverted to language more in keeping with that of the *Constitutions*. "Our rule of an hour's prayer is therefore to be adapted so that each Jesuit, guided by his superior, takes into account his particular circumstances and needs, in the light of that discerning love which St. Ignatius clearly presupposed in the Constitutions" (229).

Given his insistence on the primacy of spiritual means as outlined in the last chapter, it seems strange to find in Ignatius a seemingly laissez-faire attitude when he comes to describe the devotional practices of the formed Jesuit. To understand this paradox we need to underline the presuppositions Ignatius makes about formed Jesuits. He presumes that they will be like trained race horses, as it were, chomping at the bit to go all out in the race for union with God. He knows himself and his companions to be such. He presumes that those who come after them will have the same strong desires, the same ambition to overcome self-will in order to become one with God. These are the kind of men Ignatius had in mind when he formulated number 582 of the *Constitutions*.

Ignatius himself had experienced such a desire for union with God that he had done his body permanent harm by his early austerities and long hours of prayer. In addition, he had come to realize that the "enemy of human nature" could use these holy desires for his own purposes. Even at Manresa where long hours of prayer were a regular feature of each day, he caught the "bad angel" masquerading as an "angel of light" (*Exercises,* 332). He noticed that he was losing what little sleep he had allotted himself because of great enlightenment and consolation that came over him when he lay down to sleep. After careful examination, he says, "he came round to thinking to himself that he had a certain amount of time set aside for dealing with God...That led him to begin to doubt if these ideas were coming from the good spirit, and he came to the conclusion that it was better to leave them aside and to sleep for the allotted time; and so he did" (*Personal Writings,* p. 25). After he had returned from his pilgrimage to Jerusalem and had begun to study Latin grammar in Barcelona in preparation for higher studies in order to "help souls," he found himself hindered from memorization by a flood of spiritual insights and consolations. "And so, thinking often about this, he said to himself, 'Not even when I set myself to prayer and when I am at mass do these insights which are so vivid come to me'; and thus little by little he came to recognize that it was a temptation" (*ibid.,* p. 39). He then made a promise to his tutor not to fail to do his school work come what may. So Ignatius knew from personal experience that the evil spirit could use spiritual desires to derail a person from a path that had been discerned to be in conformity with God's will.

The Society of Jesus is an apostolic order, an order whose purpose is explained in the Formula of the Institute approved by Popes Paul III and Julius III:

> He [a Jesuit] is a member of a Society founded chiefly for this purpose: to strive especially for the defense and propagation of the faith and for the progress of souls in Christian life and doctrine, by means of public preaching, lectures, and any other ministration whatsoever of the word of God, and further by means of

the Spiritual Exercises, the education of children and unlettered persons in Christianity, and the spiritual consolation of Christ's faithful through hearing confessions and administering the other sacraments. [*Constitutions,* pp. 3-4]

Clearly Jesuits are to be "men for others," in the memorable phrase coined by Pedro Arrupe, the recent general superior, to describe alumni and alumnae of Jesuit high schools and universities. They are to spend themselves for the benefit of others. In this Formula there is no mention of the members' own spiritual health. However, in the "general examen" proposed to candidates, this lack is addressed: "The end of this Society is to devote itself with God's grace not only to the salvation and perfection of the members' own souls, but also with that same grace to labor strenuously in giving aid toward the salvation and perfection of the souls of their neighbors" [*ibid.,* p. 24]. For Ignatius the Jesuit's own spiritual health and that of those to whom he ministers go hand in hand. Since the purpose of the apostolic activity of Jesuits is the salvation and perfection of others, it stands to reason that they must also be concerned about their own salvation and perfection. *Nemo dat quod non habet* ("No one gives what he does not have") was an old Latin maxim much favored in Jesuit novitiates when Latin was the daily language. To be most effective, they must themselves be what they profess to be—men who desire union with God and who desire it from the bottom of their hearts.

Given that desire, and given that the desire has been acted upon repeatedly during their formation, Jesuits now, in Ignatius' view, must have their desire for long prayer harnessed by the needs of others. This is the tension at the heart of Jesuit spirituality, the tension between their own desire for God and their desire to help their neighbors. St. Paul wrote to the Philippians:

> For to me, living is Christ and dying is gain. If I am to live in the flesh, that means fruitful labor for me; and I do not know which I prefer. I am hard pressed between the two: my desire is to depart and be with Christ, for that is far better; but to remain in the flesh is more necessary for you. Since I am convinced of this, I know that I will remain and continue with all of you for your progress and joy

in faith, so that I may share abundantly in your boasting in Christ
Jesus when I come to you again. (1: 21 –26)

Ignatius hoped that Jesuits would experience a similar tension of
desires with regard to union with God and service of their neighbor.

We have written of the ideal, of what Ignatius hoped for in his
followers. Of course in reality, most Jesuits fall far short of this
ideal. No doubt some have excused themselves from apostolic
labors to tend to their spiritual needs. Again, some of the Portuguese and Spanish Jesuits of Ignatius' time come to mind. More
often, however, the slackening of the tension has come through an
avoidance of, even a distaste for prayer. Jesuits could justify not
praying much each day by reference to the *Constitutions*. They
were called to be apostolic. Ignatius himself once said that fifteen
minutes of prayer a day should suffice for a Jesuit. However, when
Jesuits use this argument they neglect to note that Ignatius had
said that the fifteen minutes should suffice for a *mortified* Jesuit,
that is, a Jesuit who has gained a good deal of control over his self-
indulgent tendencies. Ignatius presumed, as we noted earlier, that
Jesuits would be attracted to prayer and would have to discipline
themselves to pull themselves away from prayer for the sake of
their apostolate. At times in their history Jesuits have, it would
seem, not found prayer as attractive as Ignatius foresaw. Involvement in activity has often cooled the desire for personal prayer.

In addition to the fact that closeness to God can be daunting,
even for the person who is very attracted to such closeness, is
there something in Ignatian spirituality that might lead Jesuits,
and others, to find prayer distasteful? In the *Spiritual Exercises*
Ignatius presents a great variety of prayer methods. He describes
two different ways of praying set prayers like the "Our Father" or
"Hail Mary"—for example, to focus attention on one word or
phrase at a time. He shows how one can use one's imagination to
become part of scenes of the gospels; most of the time in a full
thirty-day retreat would be spent in such contemplation of the
gospels. He writes of the prayer of the senses, of the prayer of
examining one's conscience. The book is full of various ways to
engage in prayer.

One of these methods, however, became identified with Ignatian prayer, and this was the meditation with the three powers of the soul presented in the First Week of the Exercises for the examination of sins. In this method retreatants are told to use their memory, reasoning and will to discover how they have offended God. The use of memory, reasoning and will precedes what Ignatius calls a "colloquy," that is, a conversation with the Lord. Perhaps because this kind of meditation lent itself to the needs of preaching, this type of prayer became the norm for Jesuits and for many of those who made Ignatian retreats. So much was this the norm that in the authors' novitiate the morning hour of prayer was called "morning meditation," and was structured such that the novice was supposed to meditate for most of the hour and then begin his colloquy when the novice leader rang a bell. In this kind of regimen many Jesuits and others came to dislike, even detest such structured prayer. It is easy to see why they might use the *Constitutions* as a way to avoid what seemed excessively onerous and seemingly fruitless.

In this reading of the Ignatian tradition, prayer was hard work, not something intrinsically attractive. For many Jesuits, and for many others who imbibed this kind of Ignatian spirituality, prayer was a painful, wearying and heady process. Just recently one of us directed in an eight-day retreat an older nun who had been schooled in this tradition. She hated retreats and did not expect anything from them. The thought of spending an hour in prayer drove her to distraction. When asked why she made retreats, she answered, "Because I have to; I'm a nun." When her director suggested that she do some things that she enjoyed for a day, she replied that she would feel guilty if she did this. Obviously, she had never gotten a taste for prayer, yet her desire for closeness to God was so palpable that she shed tears when she spoke of it. But she did not believe that her desire would ever be granted. With this kind of attitude toward the exercise of prayer it is no wonder that many people avoided it if at all possible. The "head" work so often canceled their heart's need. Jesuits had an easy way to justify this avoidance, namely the statements we have taken from the *Constitutions*. More than likely, however, they did so with some feelings of guilt, feelings that showed themselves in their frequent laments that they "should pray more."

Ignatius himself found great relish in prayer and expected that others would find the same relish. Indeed, he believed that the deepest desire of the human heart was to be one with God and that this desire fueled a spiritual life that found time for prayer. He also believed that God desires to satisfy this urge and reveals himself to those who take the time to open themselves to this revelation. The *Spiritual Exercises* are based on these beliefs. Ignatius tells the director of the Exercises to "leave the Creator to work directly with the creature" [15]. He presumes that God will deal directly with each person, and that God will be experienced by each of them. This experience of God may come in a feeling of great well-being and desire for God, for example, or through a surprising remembrance that leads to gratitude for gifts received, or to sorrow for past failings. Ignatius presumes that others will have experiences such as he had which they can discern as the felt presence of God communicating to them.

In addition, Ignatius expects that God will attract people who want such communication. In the second rule for the discernment of spirits appropriate for the First Week he writes that, for those who are trying to get closer to God, "the distinctive trait of the good spirit is to give courage and strength, consolations, tears, inspirations, and quiet, making things easy and removing all obstacles, so that the person may move forward in doing good" [315]. In the Contemplation to Obtain Love he writes about "...pondering with great affection how much God our Lord has done for me, and how much He has given me of what He has; and further, how according to His divine plan, it is the Lord's wish, as far as He is able, to give me Himself" [234]. Ignatius, in other words, presumed that prayer could become very attractive because of the attractiveness of the God who is a self-revealing lover. Of course, Ignatius knew from experience that the path to this enjoyment of God may take us through some dark patches, but he was optimistic that God wants us to have this enjoyment. What he wanted to guard against for Jesuits is that such enjoyment not get in the way of service of their neighbor. If it does, he seems to believe, then it means that the bad spirit has masqueraded as an "angel of light."

In a letter to Diego Mirón, the provincial of Portugal, who had been asked along with another Jesuit to become confessors to the royal court, Ignatius indicated how he would resolve the tension between care for one's own spiritual life and for that of others. Mirón had expressed concern about the safety of his own soul if he should spend much time at court. Ignatius replied:

> My own opinion is that even the argument based on your personal safety is not relevant. Obviously if our religious profession had no other purpose but to ensure our security, and if we were supposed to subordinate the good we do to keeping clear of danger, then we would not have to live among people and have contact with them. But according to our vocation, we have contact with everyone...If we go about with our intention upright and pure,...then Christ Himself will look after us in His infinite goodness. Unless our profession clings to His powerful hand, it will not be enough to draw back from such dangers to avoid falling into them or even greater dangers. (*Personal Writings*, p 249)

Jesuits save their own souls by giving themselves to the salvation of others. They cannot allow fear of their own spiritual safety to deter them from helping souls. But, as is clear from this letter, to do this they must put their trust in the Lord. Nonetheless this service to monarchs has its downside. It could sometimes lead to corporate and individual pride among Jesuits. And it did, in fact, lead to the connection of Jesuits with the policies of unpopular monarchs, a proximate occasion for the exile of Jesuits from some countries when the unpopular monarch died or was deposed.

The one prayer that Ignatius would not allow a Jesuit, no matter how humble, to drop was the examination of conscience at least twice a day. Why? Jesuits are asked to find God in their apostolic activity. The examination of conscience gives the Jesuit the opportunity to look back over a part of the day to discover where he has been meeting God and where he may have avoided such a meeting. Ignatius himself, even to the end of his life, engaged in such examinations very often in the day. He wanted to be in tune with God's desires, and the examination was one way to achieve this.

So he demanded that each Jesuit take a short time in the middle of the day and at its end to look back over the events of the day to develop the ability to discern the presence of God's Spirit in everyday life. He wanted his companions to be in tune with God at every moment of the day, as far as this was possible.

Two saints exemplify the different ways Jesuits have lived out the tension between prayer and apostolic labor. One was the elderly widower, Brother Alphonsus Rodriguez, who after his entrance into the Society spent most of the rest of his long life as a doorkeeper at the Jesuit college on the island of Majorca. As he went to answer the door for any caller, he would say, "I'm coming, Lord," and greeted each visitor with the same smile with which he would have greeted Jesus. Peter Claver, as a novice, heard of this saintly brother and was pleased to be sent to study at Majorca so that he could engage in spiritual conversation with him. Alphonsus is the one who suggested that Peter volunteer for the missions in South America where, in Cartagena, Peter became the "slave of the black slaves for all time," as he styled himself. To read of his heroic and kindly work among the docked slave ships is to wonder at what fueled his stamina, his doggedness and his devotion. As he lay dying hundreds of Cartagenians, slave and free, crowded into his room and stripped it of everything but the bedclothes, so eager were they to have some relic of this holy man. Peter found God in this ceaseless activity of caring for the most destitute and abandoned human beings.

5. "Friends in the Lord": The Tension between Companionship and Mission

O ne of the Enlightenment philosophers is supposed to have said of Jesuits, "They meet without affection and they part without regret"—a harsh, if witty condemnation of men who are supposed to be companions of Jesus and of one another. Is it true? We have seen that the first companions had developed a deep affection for one another, an affection that withstood the tensions attributable to their differing personalities and nationalities. In fact, Ignatius described them as "friends in the Lord." Francis Xavier kept the names of the first companions near his heart and wrote movingly of his love for them. At the same time, his dear friend, Ignatius, sent him on a mission to the Indies and, in doing so, surely knew that he might never see Xavier again. How does Jesuit spirituality balance community life and apostolic need? In some ways, this tension runs parallel to the tension described in the last chapter.

The *Constitutions* do not use the word "community." It is only in relatively recent documents of the Society of Jesus that the word comes into frequent use and uses up a good deal of ink. The issue of community has obviously become a concern among Jesuits. We believe that it has done so not only because of the different times we live in, but also because Jesuits had become aware that something was amiss in the way they lived together and were seeking ways to bring back a healthy tension into the balance of community life and apostolate.

Ignatius was aware of the tension. Part VIII of the *Constitutions* is entitled: "Helps toward Uniting the Dispersed Members with Their Head and among Themselves." Ignatius writes of the difficulty of maintaining unity in dispersion, but insists on the importance of this unity. "For the Society cannot be preserved or governed or, consequently, attain the aim it seeks for the greater glory of God unless its members are united among themselves and with their head" [655].

Why should this be so? In the first place, Ignatius and the first companions conceived of the Society on the model of the disciples around Jesus. They hoped that they would experience the same love for one another that Jesus wanted to be the abiding sign of his love for his disciples (cf. John 15: 12 -17). Second, the Society was a new phenomenon in the church, and as such open to attack from those who believed its innovations contrary to standard traditions of religious life in the Roman Catholic Church. Disunity among the Jesuits would only provide fuel for such attacks. Indeed, the early Society experienced the effects of such disunity when one of the first companions, Simão Rodrigues, came close to rebellion against Ignatius on the issue of prayer in the Society and his own removal as provincial of Portugal. A number of Jesuits had to be dismissed from the province of Portugal in the aftermath. Third, the Society's mission brought it into close contact with rulers and other political leaders who often were at war with one another and with the pope. Disunity among Jesuits, who themselves were often from these warring states and cities, could destroy it.

Fourth, the Society's mission took its men into areas of controversy in the church—for example, to Germany, which was riven by religious discord—and into areas of theological controversy where heresy was easily imputed to those who held positions at variance with one's own. One clear case in point was the conflict generated by Dominicans such as Melchior Cano, who accused Jesuits of being infected with heresy. Disunity among the Jesuits would only add fuel to such fires. Fifth, the Society wanted to attract intellectually alert, strong-willed, ambitious young men to its ranks. Such men, if not strongly motivated by love for one another, could easily be at loggerheads with sad consequences for the apostolic efforts of the Society. From experience Ignatius knew the importance of unity for the preservation and effectiveness of the Society. Finally, he perceived the tension inherent in the Society between unity of hearts and dispersion for mission. How can Jesuits remain united when they are dispersed all over the world? He makes clear that the unity he speaks of is the unity of hearts, a unity based on love for one another. He then lists the means for maintaining this unity of hearts, among which are selectivity in admitting candidates, openness with superiors regarding one's inner life, expulsion of those who are divisive, obedience, union with God, and frequent communication by letter.

Ignatius was leery of admitting too many young men, "a mob," as he put it in the *Constitutions* [819], afraid that the desire to have more Jesuits would cloud the judgment of those who had the authority to admit. Late in his life he voiced one regret, that he had not been more selective in admittance. He was no less strong in his insistence that those who proved themselves divisive and unwilling to be obedient should be dismissed. Indeed, he sent a special superior to Portugal to resolve the crisis there by dismissing a large number of young Jesuits who proved recalcitrant in obeying superiors who wanted them to moderate their long hours of prayer and bizarre penances.

He insisted on obedience and on union with God as safeguards against disunity. Men who are united with God will have the humility to recognize that their judgments are at best indicative, not definitive, and will not engage in divisive discussions in the community when superiors or the majority decide an issue in a way contrary to their best judgment. Ignatius himself provides an example of this kind of humility. The King of Spain had proposed Francis Borja, the former duke of Gandía, to the pope as a cardinal. Ignatius wrote Borja a letter in which he stated, in the strongest terms, that he was convinced that God wanted him to do all in his power to prevent this from happening. He writes: "If I did not act thus, I would be (and indeed am) quite certain in myself that I would not give a good account of myself before God our Lord, rather a wholly bad one." Yet he could go on to say that he was also convinced "that while it was God's will that I should adopt a clear position, if others adopted a contrary view and you were given this dignity, there would not be any contradiction whatsoever...May God our Lord bring about—in all things, in whatever way, and at all times—His own greater praise and glory" (*Personal Writings*, p. 246). It is this kind union with God that Ignatius prizes for himself and for his companions, a union which takes seriously one's own experience as an indicator of God's will, while at the same time letting events and God be the final arbiter. Here, by the way, is an example of the dictum: "Pray as if everything depended on you; work as if everything depended on God."

It seems clear that Ignatius wanted Jesuits to love one another, to be friends in the Lord. However, this is precisely a friendship in the Lord who has a mission to accomplish in this world. Jesuits must not allow their love for one another to keep them from leaving close friends or from letting friends depart when apostolic work calls for it. Ignatius and Xavier are a good example. They clearly loved one another and enjoyed one another's company. When the King of Portugal asked for men for the Indies and the pope agreed, Ignatius decided to send Nicolá Bobadilla and Simão Rodrigues, but Bobadilla returned from one of his apostolic trips very sick. Xavier, who was acting as Ignatius' secretary, was the only other of the original companions then in Rome. Ignatius talked with Xavier and told him, "It is your task now," to which Xavier cheerfully replied, "Well, then, here I am." The depth of their affection for one another can be seen in the letters that passed between them, letters that took about a year to reach their destination. (In fact, Ignatius' last letter to Xavier, ordering him to return to Europe, was sent after Xavier had died, but before news of this event reached Rome.) It is this kind of union of hearts that Ignatius hoped for in his men. Because of his insistence on maintaining union of hearts through regular correspondence, the Jesuit missionaries have left an unparalleled record of their experiences in far-flung territories, a record that to this day is a trove for scholars seeking to understand cultures that do not have much in the way of literary remains. One example will suffice. *The Jesuit Relations,* seventy-three volumes (in the English translation) containing the annual letters sent back to France by Jesuits of the Canadian missions from 1632 until 1673, have been mined by scholars looking to understand life among the native Canadians.

What is needed for such a union of hearts? First, the companions need to be united with the Lord; they are, after all, companions of Jesus first and foremost. Second, they need to have engaged in conversations with one another about their deepest dreams, desires and hopes; in other words, they need to know one another at a rather deep level. Third, they need to put the needs of others and the good of the whole Society before their own desires for continued close companionship. Fourth, they need to keep reminding themselves of their absent friends in the Lord and to try to communicate with them. In other words, the ideal of the Jesuits is that they meet with affection, and part with regret, but that the parting be because of a greater good.

This is not an easy ideal in practice. For one thing, friendship can easily lead men to want to remain together. Such togetherness can be justified by the successes in the apostolate of their working together. Two or a group can lose the kind of openness for the greater good that needs to characterize Jesuits. In deliberations about future apostolic work they can, without knowing it, sabotage any thought of an enterprise that would separate them. Yet Jesuit spirituality requires the ability to be "indifferent" (impartial), that is, at a balance, not swayed by inordinate attachments, so that one can discern what is for "the greater glory of God."

On the other hand, because Jesuits are required to be ready to move to other places, they can hold themselves back from deep friendship to prevent the pain of separation. Men who fear this pain can maintain a certain emotional distance from their companions and thus give credence to the witticism about meeting without affection and parting without regret. Large communities where deep, personal conversations are discouraged also affect emotional closeness. In the past, fear of homoerotic attachment was often instilled in young Jesuits. For example, in the novitiates of the United States, prior to the Second Vatican Council, novices were taught to avoid "particular friendships." The novice director would admonish men if they spent too much time with certain friends, and on occasion would order two or three novices not to talk with one another for a period of time. In Germany, during the same period, Jesuit novices were forbidden to use first names or the familiar *Du,* presumably because Jesuits were to have formal, not intimate relationships with one another. Such training could and did lead to rather superficial relationships.

During most of the nineteenth and twentieth centuries talk about one's experiences of God was discouraged among Jesuits. In fact, talk of feelings in general was downplayed because feelings are "irrational." Thus, the very kind of conversation that led the first companions to become "friends in the Lord" was avoided. In many places recreation was taken in common; the whole community sat around a room and all talk was public. Conversations in these circumstances might be stimulating discussions of some relevant topic, though kept firmly away from the personal. More often they tended to be rather pedestrian: talk about the weather or sports, or complaints about the students. In other words, the creative tension that keeps a healthy balance between real companionship and apostolic involvement has been lost at times in the history of the Society.

Friendships in general are risky, difficult to develop, and often messy. It takes some time to develop the kind of trust between two persons that leads to mutual transparency with one another. Many people choose not to take the risk or to spend the time. Some Jesuits are among those who have chosen not to take the risk. In an order committed to apostolic activity, this activity can sometimes take the place of friendship. One's work for others demands all one's energies, so that there isn't time for intimate friendships with one's fellow Jesuits. Indeed, a Jesuit can justify not having time for relationships of intimacy by recourse to the apostolic purpose of the Society of Jesus. We have heard Jesuits argue in this fashion: "Look at Xavier. He lived alone most of his apostolic life; he had no time for friendships." As with the argument about prayer, however, what this argument forgets is that Xavier dearly loved his companions; apostolic activity tore him away from men whose friendship he treasured and with whom he had spent many hours in intimate conversation. He did not escape from friendship through work, as some Jesuits seem to have done.

We believe that the Society after the Second Vatican Council had to grapple with the question of community life because it was problematic. Jesuits had not learned how to communicate with one another about the deeper issues of their lives. Many were shocked by the departure of men whom they considered friends, but with whom they had had little or no communication about the struggles that led to the departure. Jesuits had to rediscover how to be friends in the Lord. It has been a difficult and messy process, yet worth the effort. As they struggle with the meaning for them of community life, they need to retain the creative tension that exists between a deeply affectionate bond with their companions and a desire to be available for those in need of their services. If that tension is present, then Jesuits will truly be "friends in the Lord."

Once again we can refer to the friendship that developed between two saints: Alphonsus Rodriguez and Peter Claver. While Peter was in Majorca, they would meet every day to engage in spiritual conversation that helped to build their friendship but did not hinder Alphonsus from encouraging Peter to volunteer for the missions in South America. In England during the Elizabethan persecutions of Catholics, Jesuits who were engaged in very dangerous underground work with Catholics tried to meet monthly, at the risk of their lives, to talk about their experiences. This is another example of how the bond of love between Jesuits was cemented by regular and profound conversation and, at the same time, enabled these men to continue their ministries that very often led to their cruel deaths.

At present Jesuits are engaged in another form of companionship—that of attempting to form a kind of community with those lay and religious colleagues with whom they work. It is also a rather confusing and difficult enterprise as Jesuits, from their own inner convictions, and encouraged by regulations of their latest congregations, seek to work together in equality and harmony in institutions that the Jesuits controlled until about thirty years ago. The Thirty-fourth General Congregation put it this way:

The Society of Jesus acknowledges as a grace of our day and a hope for the future that the laity "take an active, conscientious, and responsible part in the mission of the Church in this great moment of history." We seek to respond to this grace by offering ourselves in service to the full realization of this mission of the laity, and we commit ourselves to that end by cooperating with them in their mission.

In this companionship the same tensions will also be present, hopefully for the great good of all concerned.

6. "To Be Inwardly Free": The Tension between Obedience and Learning from Experience

n the last chapter we noted that obedience is one of the means to preserve unity singled out in the *Constitutions*. In his famous letter on obedience, sent to the Jesuits of Portugal in 1553, Ignatius declares that members of the Society of Jesus should be distinguished from other orders in the church by their obedience. He advocates obedience not only of the will but also of the intellect, so that one agrees with whatever a superior orders. Such obedience

> consists of adopting as a presupposition and belief, rather as we do when questions of faith are involved, that whatever orders are issued by the superior are really regulations of God Our Lord and expressions of His holy will. One then proceeds to do what is ordered quite blindly, without any further inquiry and with all the verve and promptness of a person wanting to obey. (*Personal Writings*, p. 258)

In the *Constitutions* Ignatius goes so far as to say that Jesuits should be willing to obey even "an indication of the superior's will without an expressed command" [547]. In the *Spiritual Exercises* he presents "Rules to follow in view of the true attitude of mind that we ought to maintain within the Church militant" (n. 352 ff.). Rule 13 states: "To maintain a right mind in all things we must always maintain that the white I see, I shall believe to be black, if the hierarchical Church so stipulates" (n. 365). When one reads such exhortations, one can wonder whether there is any place in Jesuit spirituality for learning from experience, that is, for individual discernment of spirits.

In fact, for most of the twentieth century there was not much place for it in Jesuit life. Superiors ordered, subjects obeyed. The latter may have grumbled, but they did not ask whether anything was amiss in this blind obedience. We have argued that there is, in Jesuit spirituality, a creative tension between obedience and discernment of spirits. We need to make a case for such a tension, given these strong statements about obedience.

Ignatius lived in a society that was hierarchical in its secular and sacred domains. He believed that this hierarchical order was God given. He had also been a soldier, used to the hierarchy in an army. It should not surprise us that he had such strong opinions about obedience to higher authority. Recall that in Jerusalem he concluded that God did not want him to stay in the holy places when the Franciscan provincial threatened him with excommunication if he remained. This, even though he had been convinced that God wanted him to spend his life helping souls in the land where Jesus lived. What is surprising is that Ignatius should also place such emphasis on individual discernment, and on learning from experience, and then engage in actions that seem to run counter to his own thinking on obedience.

Ignatius was convinced that the Society of Jesus was called by God to be so engaged in apostolic ventures and so mobile that it should be exempt from the obligation on all religious orders to sing the hours of the Divine Office in common each day. He fought for this exemption even when authorities wanted the Society to have choir. In addition, he believed that Jesuits should not become bishops, first, because there were so few Jesuits at the time, and second, to forestall ambition among Jesuits. When, it seemed, nothing would prevent the pope, several times, from naming one or another of the first companions a bishop, Ignatius did not immediately accept this wish as God's command. He asked all the Jesuits in Rome to pray ardently and offer Masses and wrote to influential laymen and cardinals to ask them to intercede to change the pope's mind. We have already alluded to how he acted when the pope wanted to make Francis Borja a cardinal. Obviously the practice of obedience is much more nuanced than appears from the texts we have cited.

In his own spiritual journey, Ignatius often had to rely on his personal experiences and the discernment of those experiences rather than on external authority. In Manresa he found little help with his scruples from his confessors; his final freedom from these scruples came when he discerned that they were not from God, but a temptation. After this discernment he had a vision that convinced him that he should now cease his total abstinence from eating meat. When his confessor asked him to consider whether this was a temptation, he remarks: "But he, examining the matter well, was incapable of ever being doubtful about it" (*Personal Writings*, p. 25). In these same reminiscences he recalls a number of his mystical experiences. After describing the last of these, the experience at the Cardoner River, he says that he learned more on this occasion than he learned in all his subsequent life and in all his studies. Later, as general superior, he would "explain" his reasons for many decisions about the organization of the Society by referring to his experience at the Cardoner. Learning from experience was crucially important to Ignatius.

During his studies in Spain he found himself under suspicion by those in authority. On more than one occasion he submitted his writings, the rudimentary notes that would become the *Spiritual Exercises,* to them for judgment and became frustrated that, though nothing heretical was found in them, he was forbidden from talking about the difference between mortal and venial sins until he had studied more. Study did not, it appears, force him to change his practice or doctrine. There is in Ignatius' own spiritual life a creative tension between obedience and learning from experience.

This creative tension may become clearer if we describe the way Ignatius governed, or at least desired to govern. André Ravier writes:

> According to Ignatius, there are *three preliminary steps* to the interpreting of a sign of God which result in an authentically spiritual decision: to have authority or responsibility for making the decision or participating in it, to pray to God to bestow his light, and to be inwardly free of all preference and of all personal passion. (Ravier, p. 340)

He then goes on to distinguish five phases leading to a good decision by a superior. First, he and his counselors try to get as much information as possible about the matter to be decided. Second, they examine the advantages and disadvantages of the possible decisions that could be made. Third, all of them pray for interior freedom, that is, the "indifference" of the Principle and Foundation of the *Spiritual Exercises,* and for the light of the Holy Spirit. Fourth, after the counselors give their opinion, the superior gives his opinion and then weighs the matter once again before God; no matter what the majority of the counselors believe, the superior must decide before God and his own conscience. Fifth, once he has made his decision he must then again offer it to God in prayer asking for confirmation of his decision. "A decision made in this manner then became for Ignatius the will of God. Unless there were obviously contrary signs, he carried it out regardless of cost" (*ibid.,* p. 341).

Ignatius develops this methodology in the section of the *Constitutions* where he takes up the dismissal of a novice. To get a flavor of Ignatius' way of governing it might be good to cite the whole passage. The reader will note the great care for the individual inculcated by Ignatius at a time when stern harshness might tend to prevail. We can presume that the novice has given ample cause for the dismissal.

1. With those who must be dismissed, that manner ought to be employed which before God our Lord is likely to give greater satisfaction to the one who dismisses as well as to the one dismissed and to the others within and without the house. For the satisfaction of the one who dismisses, for the causes mentioned above, three points should be observed.

2. The first point to be observed is that he should pray and order prayers in the house for this intention (although the person's identity remains unknown), that God our Lord may make his holy will known in this case.

3. The next point is that he should confer with one or more persons in the house who seem more suitable and hear their opinions.

4. The third point is that, ridding himself of all affection and keeping before his eyes the greater divine glory and the common good,

and the good of the individual as far as possible, he should weigh the reasons on both sides and make his decision to dismiss or not.

5. For the satisfaction of the one dismissed, three further points ought to be observed. One, pertaining to the exterior, is that as far as possible he should leave the house without shame or dishonor and take with him whatever belongs to him.

6. The second point, pertaining to the interior, is to try to send him away with as much love and charity for the house and as much consoled in our Lord as is possible.

7. The last, pertaining to his personal condition, is to try to guide him in taking up some other good means of serving God, in religious life or outside it as may seem more conformable to his divine will, assisting him with advice and prayers and whatever in charity may seem best.

8. Likewise, for the satisfaction of the others inside and outside the house, three things ought to be observed. One is that everything possible should be done to ensure that no one is left troubled in spirit by the dismissal; satisfactory grounds for it can be given to whoever needs it, touching as little as possible upon faults in the person which are not public (even if he has them).

9. A second is that they should not be left disaffected or with a bad opinion in his regard, as far as this is possible. Rather, they should have compassion for him and love him in Christ and recommend him in their prayers to the Divine Majesty, that God may deign to guide him and have mercy on him. [218–229]

The practice of obedience in Jesuit governance, obviously, is not supposed to be authoritarian and arbitrary. Moreover, Ignatius wants superiors to act with love, even when they must do something painful for another.

Jesuit obedience must also be seen in the context of the account of conscience that is a hallmark of Jesuit spirituality. The *Constitutions* stipulate that at least once a year (or oftener, if necessary) each Jesuit open his heart to his provincial superior. He is asked to put all his trust in superiors and to keep "nothing exterior or interior hidden from" them and to desire them "to be informed about everything, so that the superiors may be able to direct them in everything along the path of salvation and perfection" [551].

The purpose of this full disclosure of oneself is apostolic. Ignatius wanted superiors to know the reality of their men so that they could make appropriate assignments. Among the things that he expected Jesuits to reveal in this account of conscience were their apostolic desires, the weaknesses and temptations to which they were prone, the strengths they possessed, their health, and so on. The superior needed to know his men in order to make good apostolic decisions as to how best to deploy them. He would be less likely to put a man in a job that might be injurious to him or to those with whom he was to work if he knew everything about him. But he could also learn from the man something about God's will. In fact, according to the *Memoriale* of Gonçalves da Câmara, Ignatius made every effort to know the desires and inclinations of men who were prayerful and humble, being willing to follow their inclinations in assigning them (Ravier, p. 324).

In other words, Ignatius also expected that God's will could be made manifest through the experience of the men themselves. The idea of "blind obedience" has to be understood in the light of the way Ignatius envisioned the mode of decision-making by superiors and subjects. The superior did not have a direct pipeline to God. Everyone needed to work together to discover the best way to act in any given situation.

In addition to the account of conscience, the *Constitutions* reveal another characteristic of Jesuit obedience and discernment. Frequently, after detailed instructions about how one is to act, one reads that these prescriptions are to be tailored according to the "circumstances of times, places, persons, and other such factors" [351]. Ignatius realized that he could not foresee all the circumstances that might necessitate adjustments in how one acted. Jesuits are expected to use their discretion in applying the law, and to be discerning even in matters that are legislated by the *Constitutions* or mandated by superiors.

Jesuit obedience requires that Jesuits be men of prayer and abnegation, men who are sincerely seeking God's will in all that they do. It also requires that they be men who have learned to discern the chaff from the wheat in their own experience through steady use of the twice-daily examination of conscience and application of the rules for discernment of spirits. They are not expected to be automatons who have no mind and will of their own; rather they are to be men who believe in practice that God communicates directly with them, as with superiors and everyone else. They are also to be men who are humble enough to recognize their own fallibility and, as a result, who do not become so enamored of their own discernment that they cannot abide any contradiction. What Ignatius wrote to Francis Borja in the matter of the cardinal's hat should characterize every Jesuit; after he has done his best to get across what he has discerned, he needs to leave the rest to God.

In the honest and open interchange between superior and subject Jesuits expect to discover how to be in tune with God's intention in this world. This a far cry from the caricature of Jesuit obedience often encountered. Jesuits at their best live with the creative tension between obedience and personal discernment, expecting that in this creative tension they will find themselves attuned to God's intention.

Of course, the tension can become flaccid. For most of the last century there was little attention paid to the implications of the account of conscience in Jesuit life. Jesuits did see their provincials once a year, but these sessions were often perfunctory. Provincials, for the most part, were more interested in the externals of performance of one's duties than in the interior experiences of one's mind and heart. Subjects were content to get in and out without a reprimand. Assignments were rarely discussed with the individual before they were made. In fact, most men found out what they would be doing for the next academic year when the assignments were posted on the bulletin board on a given summer day. The perfunctory nature of the account of conscience prior to the rediscovery of its centrality to Jesuit obedience in the last quarter of the twentieth century is understandable. Provinces, especially in the United States, consisted of large numbers of men. Because of the press of numbers it would have been humanly impossible for a provincial to hear the account of conscience as Ignatius envisioned it, even if he wanted to do so. In fact, when the account of conscience was restored as central to Jesuit obedience after the Second Vatican Council, provincials of the larger provinces had to be assisted by vice provincials who could hear the account of conscience. In addition, during most of the nineteenth and twentieth centuries Catholic theology and practice did not value experience as a locus for finding God's will, or even God's presence; God's will was discovered by listening to authorities. This was the general atmosphere for Jesuit obedience. Individual discernment had almost no role to play in it.

The tension can also lose its force and creativity in Jesuit spirituality if superiors lose credibility as a source of finding God's will. This can happen if superiors themselves lose confidence in their authority and, for example, let the majority opinion of their counselors rule them even when, from the account of conscience, they know things that make the opinion of the majority untenable. It can also happen if superiors cede all the power of decision-making to the individual. Finally, it can happen if they are perceived as men who do not take prayer and discernment of spirits seriously. From the side of Jesuits who are not superiors, the tension can lose its creative force if they do not trust superiors and do not speak honestly with them in the account of conscience. The same can happen if they are not free of inordinate attachment to their own desires for a particular position or locale.

As noted earlier, Jesuit spirituality thrives on the tension between obedience to superiors and individual discernment of spirits. In this tension Jesuits, at their best, expect that they will discover God's will, and that they will be attuned to God's intention in this world.

An example may illustrate this tension and its resolution. Robert Drinan, S.J. had discerned a call to run for Congress in a district in Massachusetts. He was given permission by his provincial superior and won election. He served in Congress for ten years, from 1970 to 1980, often a focus of intense feelings pro and con among Catholics. In 1980 Fr. Arrupe, the general superior, ordered him not to stand for reelection, and Drinan called a press conference to announce that he would not seek reelection at the bidding of his superiors. In his remarks he said: "I am proud and honored to be a priest and Jesuit. As a person of faith, I must believe that there is work for me to do which somehow will be more important than the work I am required to leave. I undertake this new pilgrimage with pain and prayers." He has gone on to a distinguished career at Georgetown Law School and as a writer without showing a trace of bitterness, even though the order from Fr. Arrupe was a hard pill to swallow.

7. "A Special Obedience": The Tension between the Center and the Periphery in the Church

n chapter 2 we noted that the first companions had decided to put themselves at the disposal of the pope when they could not make the trip to Jerusalem. When they formed a religious order, they added to the three vows of poverty, chastity and obedience a fourth vow, namely a promise of "special obedience to the sovereign pontiff in regard to the missions." This vow earned the Jesuits the sobriquet "the pope's army," not a particularly apt term. As we noted, the first companions introduced this vow as a way to make themselves more available for missions anyplace in the world without being biased by their own nationality and ethnicity. The vow caused controversy at the time of the founding of the Society, some cardinals arguing that the vow is superfluous because all Catholics are bound by obedience to the pope. Ignatius, however, was adamant, and considered this vow one of the pillars upon which the Society stood. The practice of this vow has been the source of tension and controversy in the history of the Society.

First, the vow embroiled the Society in controversy because the pope in those times was the ruler of the papal states and, as such, often at war with other countries, including nominally Catholic ones, for example, Spain and France. Jesuits at work in these countries found themselves torn in their loyalties and accused of siding with the nation's enemies. One pope, Paul IV, who mistrusted Spaniards and engaged in war with Spain, was suspicious of Jesuits, not only because of misunderstandings with Ignatius when both were in Venice, but also because so many of them, especially the leaders, were Spanish.

Second, the papal curia and the popes themselves were considered in need of reformation because of rampant nepotism, venality and sexual misconduct. Ignatius and the first Jesuits realized the need for this reformation but also found themselves defending papal prerogatives, a defense which engendered disaffection among some Catholic reformers.

Third, and more crucial, Jesuits could, in carrying out their missions in faraway places, make decisions that the pope and his curia found insupportable when they heard about them. Jesuit obedience, such as we have explained it in the previous chapter, is not easily understood, and Jesuits who use their own prudence to make apostolic decisions in distant countries open themselves to charges of being disobedient. One notable case in history was the Chinese rites controversy. The Jesuits in China came to the conclusion that some of the Chinese ways of honoring ancestors and Confucius were not idolatrous and could be used by converted Catholics. Others thought the Jesuits wrong and eventually convinced Pope Clement XI to condemn the Jesuit practice in 1704. His successor, Innocent XIII, accused the Jesuits of disobedience against this decree and harshly reprimanded the general superior for not doing enough to enforce the prohibition of the Chinese rites. Later he implicitly acknowledged that such was not the case and revoked the penalties to be imposed.

Fourth, the vow of obedience to the pope could be interpreted to mean that Jesuits are obliged to support the pope no matter what the issue might be. Jesuits themselves have argued for this position and have considered other Jesuits who disagreed as disobedient or, at least, as misguided. We need to look carefully at this thorny matter.

We can approach an understanding of a Jesuit's understanding of the fourth vow by noting Ignatius' own comments on the matter in the *Constitutions*. In the "General Examen," a document to be presented to those who are in first probation, he says of this vow: "This is a vow to go anywhere His Holiness will order, whether among the faithful or the infidels, without pleading an excuse and without requesting any expenses for the journey, for the sake of matters pertaining to the worship of God and the good of the Christian religion" [n. 7]. In Part V of the *Constitutions,* a note after describing the formula of the vow states: "The entire purport of this fourth vow of obedience to the pope was and is with regard to missions; and this is how the bulls [the papal decrees founding the Society] should be understood where they speak of this obedience in all that the sovereign pontiff may command and wherever he may send one, and so on" [529]. It is clear that the vow is about mission and mobility. Ignatius wanted Jesuits ready to go anywhere the pope wished to send them, presuming that the pontiff had the more universal view. Ignatius followed the intent of this vow in sending Xavier to the Indies and two others of the first companions, Salmerón and Broët, on a very dangerous mission to Ireland by way of Scotland. That Ignatius did not see the vow as meaning the Jesuits had to accept anything the pope wished is shown in the way he resisted the popes who wanted to make Jesuits bishops or Francis Borja cardinal, as we noted in the last chapter. He marshaled all the help he could get to keep the pope from doing this.

There is no doubt, however, that from the beginning Jesuits were inclined toward what became known in the nineteenth century as ultramontanism, the tendency to defend the papacy and papal rights against any encroachment on its religious and secular authority, either from within the church or from without. After all, they owed their existence to the papacy and used the papal bulls as protection when they came under fire. For example, in Ignatius' own time the Society ran into trouble in France, a country ever jealous of its prerogatives as the "eldest daughter of the church." In 1556 the bishop of Paris and the Theological Faculty condemned the Jesuits in no uncertain terms: "This Society appears to be a danger to the Faith, a disturber of the peace of the church, destructive of monastic life, and destined to cause havoc rather than edification" (O'Malley, p. 289). Ignatius' response was to argue that calling into question the Holy See's right to grant pastoral privileges to religious orders was "against the faith" (*ibid.,* 302). The tendency to overemphasize the prerogatives of the papacy showed itself again when Diego Laínez, Ignatius' successor as general superior, argued at the Council of Trent that a bishop's jurisdiction derived not from his office, but from the papacy, an opinion shared by Ignatius when he was alive, but one that was defeated at that Council.

At the same time, Laínez and other Jesuits worked strenuously for the reform of the papal curia. Laínez himself was asked by Paul IV in 1556 to help him in the reform of the scandal of simony in the curia. He wrote a tract that made the papacy's sins, mistakes and scandals responsible for the loss of northern Europe to the Catholic Church. His defense of the papacy's prerogatives did not prevent him from a strong indictment of the papacy to a pope who was not well disposed to the Society. The relationship of the Society to the papacy is a rather nuanced one, even if in its history it has been on the side of those who defended the papacy against attacks on its religious authority.

Pope Clement XIV suppressed the Society of Jesus in 1773. This final indignity followed the forcible exile of all Jesuits first from Portugal and all its territories, then from France and finally from Spain and all its territories. These same countries put such intense pressure on the pope that he finally succumbed. There are many reasons for the enmity against the Jesuits, not the least its own sins and failings. Giulio Cordara, S.J., a close friend of the general superior Lorenzo Ricci and of many cardinals, wrote an account of the suppression to his brother, a book that has just been published in English. Near the end of the book he singles out Jesuit pride as a reason why God might have wanted the suppression of the Society, a pride that showed itself in the very way Jesuit novices were trained. However, he also makes clear that court ministers to the Bourbon kings and to the king of Portugal hated the Jesuits for a number of reasons, but one reason especially stands out. Jesuits were staunch defenders of the papacy at a time when these countries were trying to assert their own prerogatives against papal authority.

In addition, they were confessors for monarchs in these countries, and thus, in the popular imagination, tied in with their policies. Recall the words of Ignatius to Diego Mirón about disregarding his own safety for the sake of the desire to help souls, when asked to become confessor at the Spanish court. Taking on this apostolic work led to great danger to the Society itself, not only because closeness to power breeds arrogance, but also because one can become associated with the policies of those in power and lose a great deal when these policies become unpopular. Thus the spirituality of tensions can jeopardize the very existence of the order. This is true not only when Jesuits allow the tensions to become weak and some Jesuits become seduced by one side or the other of the tension, but also when the tensions are operative, because then Jesuits can be caught in the middle of strong political and religious conflicts.

Jesuits, for the most part, responded admirably and with great courage to this suppression, obeying the papal order without becoming alienated from the church. Lorenzo Ricci, the general superior at the time, was imprisoned in the papal prison, Castel Sant'Angelo, where he was cruelly treated. Just before his death in that prison he was finally allowed to receive holy communion. As the priest held the host, Ricci read a statement in which he affirmed, knowing that he was about to face his God, that the Society had given no cause for its suppression and he no cause for his imprisonment. Most Jesuit priests became diocesan priests, and many of these maintained ties with one another for years. That obedience to a papal order exerted strong pressures on Jesuits showed itself in the way Jesuits in Prussia and Russia reacted when the rulers of these countries refused to accept the papal decree of suppression for their territories. The Jesuit provincials were in a quandary and asked for enlightenment from Rome. In Prussia the issue was resolved when King Frederick and the Vatican came to a diplomatic resolution that the Society would be dissolved there.

In Russia Catherine the Great adamantly refused to allow the promulgation of the decree of suppression in spite of the provincial's insistence that the Jesuits were caught in a conscience bind because of their vow of obedience. She did not want to lose these admirable schoolmasters. The provincial appealed to the pope, Pius VI, explaining the difficult situation they were in and asking him to indicate that he was not displeased with them. The pope's verbal reply was deliberately enigmatic or ambivalent enough that the Society could in good conscience continue to exist in the persons of the Jesuits in Russia and those who affiliated with them. Finally, the pope gave his explicit approbation of the Society's status in Russia. The Society continued and even began to thrive in the lands ruled by Catherine.

Restored in 1814, the Society of Jesus welcomed back those members who were still alive. Rather quickly, large numbers of new recruits entered and had to be trained. The formation of these new men tended to focus on only one side of the tensions we have been discussing in this book. Obedience was stressed, but individual discernment of spirits was overlooked, for example. And the interpretation of the fourth vow tended to stress complete loyalty to the papacy. In the nineteenth and early twentieth centuries the papacy was allied with the weakening monarchies of Europe against the rising tides of nationalism and democracy. Thus the restored Society found itself strongly tied in with the papacy and with these monarchies. In the secular world of Europe this meant that Jesuits were often aligned with the "right" in opposition to the "left." In the church the papacy was fighting to keep political control of the papal states against the forces aiming at the unification of Italy under one secular government. Jesuits weighed in to defend the pope's prerogatives. In addition, popes were waging an increasingly bitter battle to centralize church authority. At the First Vatican Council Pius IX, with the help of Jesuits, among others, saw to it that papal infallibility was defined as dogma. To understand some of the turmoil of the latter part of the twentieth century, it is important to keep in mind that the Society of Jesus was considered the bulwark of the papacy and, in some cases, of governments that were desperately trying to save themselves from the forces of democratization and of collectivization.

At the same time, early in the twentieth century, some Jesuits were engaged in enterprises that put them at odds with the prevailing orthodoxy and got them in trouble not only with the Roman Curia, but also with general superiors. In France and other countries, centers for social analysis began to question the present social order that was alienating the working class. Jesuits in the United States involved themselves in union work and in schools for the laboring classes. Jesuits were involved in the Modernist controversy early in the twentieth century, and some of them were declared heretics and left the church. Jesuits have never been a monolithic group of like-thinkers.

With this as background, it might be helpful in understanding Jesuit spirituality to look at some of the defining moments of the relationship between the papacy and the Jesuits since the Second Vatican Council. Some Jesuits played key roles in that Council itself. Henri de Lubac of France, Karl Rahner of Germany and John Courtney Murray of the United States, for example, were called in as theological experts and were instrumental in writing some of the groundbreaking documents of that Council. All three had been under clouds of suspicion for their theological writings in the years after the Second World War. These Jesuits and others were part of the ferment in theology that had prepared the ground for the breakthroughs of the Council, in spite of the atmosphere of suspicion and fear that characterized the Catholic Church in the aftermath of the Modernist crisis early in the century. The decrees of the Council and its call to religious congregations to renew themselves, in the light of their charismatic roots and the needs of modern times, opened the doors to questions about some time-honored ways of thinking and of doing things in the church. A cultural and religious sea change took place in the years following the Council, and the church was riven by conflicts between those who welcomed the changes and those who found them insupportable. Those of us who lived through those times may not have been aware of how tumultuous they were, comparable in many ways, no doubt, to the changes that the church experienced during the Reformation and its aftermath. What sometimes made the changes disconcerting was that they came from inside the church itself and not from some external and hostile force, as at the time of the Reformation.

Jesuits were caught up in this sea change. Within a short time the face of the Society changed so radically that some questioned whether it was still the same Society of Jesus. The Thirty-first General Congregation in 1965-66 and the Thirty-second in 1975 were the Society's attempts to do what the Council had asked of all religious congregations. These congregations, especially the Thirty-second, caused tensions within the Society and led to some serious differences between the Society and the popes.

At the Thirty-second General Congregation the neuralgic issue that caused Pope Paul VI to intervene personally in the proceedings was the question of who could pronounce the four vows of the professed Jesuit. In the discussions among Jesuits around the world prior to the Congregation, a consensus had emerged that it was time to change the restrictions regarding qualifications for the "professed" members and to admit men who were not priests, that is, fully formed Jesuit brothers, to final profession. The pope was not happy with this turn of events and privately indicated as much to Father Arrupe, the general superior. But Arrupe and the delegates believed that they should, at least, discuss the question because of the overwhelming number of requests that had come from the official province meetings prior to the Congregation. In addition they judged that they were free to do so, in the spirit of Jesuit obedience that allows for proper representation to a superior when one has reasons to raise questions about an order. They proceeded to the discussion and to a straw vote. When Pope Paul heard of it, he got quite angry and informed the members that they had acted contrary to his will. This intervention unnerved the delegates, some of whom afterward spoke of the trauma they experienced at being perceived as disobedient. That they felt this way indicates how deeply the fourth vow had sunk into their consciousness. Moreover, as obedient Jesuits they dropped the issue.

Paul VI's successor, John Paul I, who lived only a month after his election, had prepared a talk to a gathering of Jesuits in which he indicated his hesitations about some of the activities of Jesuits and his concern about where the Society was headed. His successor, John Paul II, harbored the same misgivings. When, in 1980, Pedro Arrupe, with the agreement of his consultors and the provincials of the Society throughout the world, decided to step down as general superior for reasons of age and health, Pope John Paul II told him that he wanted time to think it over. He was, however, soon afterwards the victim of an attempted assassination and did not respond to Arrupe. In August 1981, Arrupe suffered a debilitating stroke returning from a trip to Asia. According to the

Constitutions, Arrupe appointed one of his assistants, Vincent O'Keefe, vicar general. On October 6, 1981, Pope John Paul II showed how much he then mistrusted the Jesuits by appointing his own personal delegate, Paolo Dezza, S.J., to run the Society. That he foresaw this intervention as possibly lasting for some time is indicated by the fact that he appointed Giuseppe Pittau, the provincial of Japan, as Dezza's deputy and successor if Dezza should become incapacitated. (Dezza was nearly blind and over eighty at the time.) This intervention was a shocking blow to the Society. The way Jesuits reacted is an indication of their spirituality and their understanding of the fourth vow.

There were some Jesuits who applauded the pope's intervention. One man said that he and some of his friends hoped that Father Dezza would change all of Father Arrupe's appointments, namely all the provincials at the time. But the great majority were stunned and wondered what the Society had done to merit such a public humiliation. It was made clear to all Jesuits that Father Arrupe and his assistants expected obedience to and respect for the pope's decision, to see it as God's will at this time. To our knowledge no Jesuits left the Society or the church as a result. Jesuit reactions ranged from sorrow to sadness to shock to anger, but no Jesuit made any public statements attacking the papal action. Some German Jesuits, including Karl Rahner, wrote a respectful letter to the pope indicating that they did not understand his action but would obey him. The provincials of the United States wrote a similar letter. Surprisingly, the ordinary governance of the Society went on without any changes of orientation under the regime of Father Dezza. Dezza called a meeting of the provincials from around the world at which the pope spoke rather warmly and indicated that soon a General Congregation to elect a new general superior would take place. This happened in September, 1983. Contrary to some expectations, the pope did not intervene, as had at least one previous pope, to indicate his choice for the new general superior. On the first ballot Peter-Hans Kolvenbach, a Dutchman who had worked for years in the Middle East, was elected. At that Congregation Pedro Arrupe was greeted with great warmth by the delegates, and Pope John Paul II himself spoke highly of him and approvingly of the way the Society had reacted to his [the pope's] intervention. The years since 1983 have witnessed a return to normalcy in the relationship of the Society with the papacy.

This does not mean that all is now smooth sailing. These are difficult times in the church as all of us try to find our way in the throes of post-modernity. Jesuit scholars have come under fire for their theological writing. For example, in 1999 the Vatican Congregation for the Doctrine of the Faith began an investigation of Jacques Dupuis, a noted Jesuit professor at the Gregorian University in Rome whose book, *Toward a Christian Theology of Religious Pluralism,* tried to work out a theological understanding of how salvation is attained by those who belong to non-Christian religions. For over two years Dupuis was forbidden to teach while the investigation and trial went on. It was a very distressing time for this elderly Jesuit, to be accused of deviating from the Catholic faith. In 2001 he was cleared of this charge. That Jesuits can still respectfully speak the truth as they see it, even to the pope himself, was shown by a strong editorial written in the aftermath of this investigation by the editors of *America,* the weekly magazine of opinion edited by the Jesuits of the United States, in the issue of April 9, 2001, which ended with this paragraph:

> The inquisitorial methods of the Congregation for the Doctrine of the Faith are out of date and do not respect human rights. They should be dismantled without delay. There is enough intelligence in the Catholic community, created and sustained by God's Spirit, to find better ways to safeguard the faith. Pope John Paul II has quite bravely apologized for the treatment of Galileo and other sins of the church, but along with confession should come a firm purpose of amendment.

Jesuits at their best are obedient to the pope while at the same time not puppets that have no minds of their own. They believe that God's Spirit speaks in and through all of God's people and that the institutions of the church, hierarchy, religious and lay, need to be attentive to this voice. Their spirituality again shows itself as one of creative tension.

8. "For the Ultimate End": Creative Tensions in the Use of This World's Goods

n the *Constitutions* Ignatius writes of poverty: "Poverty, as the strong wall of the religious institute, should be loved and preserved in its integrity as far as this is possible with God's grace." In order to safeguard this strong wall he requires that all who pronounce the vows of profession "should promise not to take part in altering what pertains to poverty in the *Constitutions,* unless it be in some manner to make it more strict" [553]. Ignatius wrestled with the question of poverty as he was writing the *Constitutions.* The only part that remains of what was apparently his extensive spiritual diary covers the period from February 1544 until February 1545 when he was trying to decide whether even the churches of the Society should have no fixed income, but subsist on alms. Ignatius agonized over this question because he was being moved to change something that all the first companions had earlier agreed upon, namely that the churches could have fixed income, a decision made in order to make these churches viable. The diary is an extraordinary document that reveals an intense spiritual life characterized by inner visions of the Trinity and tears of great consolation. Because of his experiences he concluded that the Society should not have any fixed income, even for its churches. The Society would live on alms, and Jesuits would not accept any salaries or other remuneration for any of its ministries. Gratuity of ministries would be the norm for all Jesuits.

Anyone who has gone to a Jesuit school or requested a funeral Mass at a Jesuit church may wonder what has happened since Ignatius penned the *Constitutions.* Jesuits charge tuition, ask for a stipend for certain Masses, receive salaries. Have the Jesuits fallen away from the poverty of their founding documents? Has the firm wall of their religious institute been breached? These are the questions we address in this chapter.

The early Jesuits gloried in the gratuity of their ministries; they found great spiritual consolation in living on alms. They also won the esteem of those to whom they ministered as a result of this kind of poverty. They were seen as different from many other priests who seemed to use ordination as a way to get ahead economically. In the early years after the Society's founding they had few stable houses, and these were professed houses, which were required to live on alms alone. But soon the success of their ministry drew young men to want to enter the Society. Many of these recruits needed formation and education, and the best way to do this seemed to be to set up schools run by Jesuits themselves. In addition, as we noted in the second chapter, the request of the Viceroy of Sicily that the Jesuits inaugurate a school in Messina for lay students led to the founding of a number of such schools in Ignatius' own lifetime. In Rome itself Ignatius founded the Roman College, later to become the Gregorian University. These schools were to be, like all Jesuit ministries, tuition-free for the students, but that meant that they needed to be endowed. By necessity Ignatius and the Jesuits became fund-raisers. One of Ignatius' great headaches, in fact, was the financial situation of the Roman College whose existence was always in jeopardy, until it was endowed by Pope Gregory XIII. With the need to raise money for endowments for the colleges and for the training of young Jesuits, the Society, even in Ignatius' time, faced the question of how to remain poor while doing everything possible to get the wealthy to aid them.

From the very beginning this need for funds put Jesuits in touch with wealthy patrons, at least some of whom led less than exemplary lives. Some pious people were scandalized by the fact that Jesuits consorted with people of dubious morals. For example, the bishop of one of the Spanish dioceses in the time of Ignatius had a mistress and six children. He was won over by a Jesuit and gave the Jesuits his mistress's house, but did not give up his "sinful ways." There were whispers: "The Jesuits carried Baal together with the Ark of the Lord." Ignatius was untroubled, writing a letter to the prelate thanking him for his generosity. Some Jesuits as well seem to have been scandalized by the contacts they had to make. To one, Ignatius wrote in 1549:

You seem to hold that the use of natural helps or resources, and taking advantage of the favor of man, for ends that are good and acceptable to our Lord, is to bend the knee to Baal. Rather, it would seem that the man who thinks that it is not good to make use of such helps or to employ this talent along with others which God has given him, under the impression that mingling such helps with the higher ones of grace produces a ferment or evil concoction has not learned well to order all things to God's glory and to find a profit in and with all these things for the ultimate end, which is God's honor and glory. (Clancy, pp. 21-22)

This admonition reminds us of Ignatius' letter to Diego Mirón who hesitated to become the confessor to the royal court of Spain because of danger to his soul.

We get an indication of how pressing financial matters were and of his mind-set in this postscript to a letter to the Jesuit rector, Alfonso Roman, in Zaragoza, Spain:

Please bear with my talking of financial matters as if they had top priority. As I have more than 160 hungry mouths to feed, not to mention the upkeep of the buildings, it is quite true that the letters likely to bring me most comfort will be letters of credit. They help me run the colleges, so I run after them for the colleges' sake—primarily out of holy obedience that has placed me in this and similar affairs. May Christ Our Lord accept all this activity! It is certainly true that even if obedience were not there to make me see how important all this is, it would be enough to consider how great and how outstanding in God's service this work is, for which such activity is very necessary. (*Personal Writings*, p. 266)

Ignatius had no qualms about asking for money, even from men who led rather unsavory lives, because he was convinced that God had called the Society to engage in the apostolate of education and that the work was very fruitful.

He was also concerned about the health of his men in Rome. Because the air was unhealthy in that city, he bought a country house outside the city so that Jesuits could get away for the sake of their health. Indeed the very last words of the *Constitutions* speak of the need to preserve the health of Jesuits with this note: "For this purpose it is expedient that attention should be given to having the houses and colleges in healthy locations with pure air and not in those characterized by the opposite" [827]. Poverty was measured by the needs of the apostolate; it was not an end in itself.

Jesuits embrace poverty as a means of helping souls. At their best, they try to follow the lead of the "Principle and Foundation" of the *Spiritual Exercises*.

> The human person is created to praise, reverence and serve God Our Lord, and by so doing to save his or her soul. The other things on the face of the earth are created for human beings in order to help them pursue the end for which they are created. It follows from this that one must use other created things in so far as they help towards one's end, and free oneself from them in so far as they are obstacles to one's end. To do this we need to make ourselves indifferent to all created things, provided the matter is subject to our free choice and there is no prohibition. Thus as far as we are concerned, we should not want health more than illness, wealth more than poverty, fame more than disgrace, a long life more than a short one, and similarly for all the rest, but we should desire and choose only what helps us more towards the end for which we are created. [n. 23]

As long as their eyes are on God and the needs of God's people, Jesuits can be discerning in the use of this world's goods. But if they lose this focus, they can go badly astray, as the example of Antoine Lavalette, mentioned at the end of the first chapter, demonstrates. Even with their eyes on God and the needs of God's people, they need to be wary of the "bad angel" who can "assume the form of 'an angel of light'" [*Sp. Ex.* n. 332]. That is, they can easily be seduced into rationalizations that allow them almost any luxury as necessary for the apostolate. But Ignatius would tell them to remain within the tension of trying to discern how to use material goods and money for the good of souls and not to escape from the tension by resort to radical poverty.

But we still must answer the question of whether the Society of Jesus has deviated from the intentions of its founder with regard to poverty. After the restoration of the Society in 1814, the Society faced the daunting task of beginning over again all its apostolic enterprises. Most of its former schools were irretrievably lost. In many countries of Europe and South America one finds magnificent public buildings that were originally Jesuit schools. These were taken over by the government when the Society was suppressed and not returned after the restoration. Finding donors who would found and completely endow new schools proved next to impossible. Tuition had to be charged. In addition, to support their works at home and abroad Jesuits found that they had to take stipends for Masses offered. They appealed to the popes for a dispensation from their vow of gratuity of education ministries, and the dispensation was granted and was continually renewed for over a century.

However, this need for a dispensation bothered Jesuits. They wondered how this practice could be squared with the vow of the professed Jesuits not to relax poverty. And they wondered how a General Congregation could engage in a discussion of this matter since the vow forbade taking part in any discussion of altering poverty unless it was to make it stricter. The Thirty-first General Congregation (1965-66) grasped this nettle by interpreting the vow in this statement: "To bring about an innovation in regard to poverty means to relax it by admitting any revenues or assets for the use of the community, whether with a view to the sacristy, maintenance, or any other purpose, apart from the case of colleges and houses of probation." It went on to say that "solemnly professed are obliged only to this: not to grant a stable income [that is, one that comes from an endowment] to professed houses and independent residences..." (Decree 18, n. 14).

At the time of this Congregation most Jesuits lived and worked at schools and so were exempt from the strict poverty enjoined by the *Constitutions*. These Jesuit schools and the Jesuit communities attached to them were single corporations; that is, all income to the school came to the single corporation which was the school and the Jesuit community and was used both for the upkeep of the Jesuits and for the school itself. Jesuits did not receive salaries for their work. Tuition was kept as low as possible for the survival and growth of the school and the community. In good times both thrived; but in bad times superiors worried where the money for the next bill would come from. Nonetheless, the buildings on Jesuit campuses built prior to the early 1970s were paid for by the sweat of the Jesuits who worked at these campuses. The revenues did not enrich the community itself but were used to develop the institutions.

Beginning in the late 1960s in the United States, first the universities and later the high schools began a process of legally separating the Jesuit community from the corporation that was the institution. With time, through legal agreements binding on both entities, most Jesuit schools became corporations separate from the corporations that constituted the Jesuit communities. Jesuits now were on the books for salaries, although the salaries did not go to the individual Jesuit, but to the community. At the end of each fiscal year the Jesuit community made significant contributions to the school from its surplus after expenditures. Some communities accumulated considerable funds that were invested for the good of the community and for apostolic uses, especially for the school. Questions of poverty continued to trouble the Society, not only with regard to the lifestyle of some of these communities, but also with regard to how the schools which, when originally founded often served the children of immigrant Catholics, could still serve the poor.

The Thirty-second General Congregation (1974 –75), whose Decree Four committed the Society to work for justice as a constituent of the promotion of the faith, proposed a solution to the vexed question of institutional poverty by requiring separate incorporation of the Jesuit community from the apostolic institution. The institution could have endowments and receive income. But the Jesuit communities were equated with the original meaning of "houses of the professed" and as such could have no stable revenues from invested capital. This meant that no Jesuit community could invest its surplus in order to insure revenue for the following year or years. Every community was required to distribute its surplus at the end of each fiscal year. The Congregation

66

allowed the community to keep a certain amount of its surplus for contingency purposes, up to the amount of the next year's budget. Gradually in the years since this Congregation these proposals have been implemented.

In the United States the Jesuit provincials have mandated that communities not keep in reserve more than twenty-five percent of its annual budget. In addition to this structural solution, the Congregation's Decree Four urged solidarity with the poor whose plight most often was due to unjust social structures. To meet the demands of this apostolic thrust the Society needed to reform its practice of poverty. "Jesuits will be unable to hear the 'cry of the poor' unless they have greater personal experience of the miseries and distress of the poor...Our communities will have no meaning or sign value for our times, unless by their sharing of themselves and all they possess, they are clearly seen to be communities of charity and of concern for each other and all others" (Decree 12, n. 5). So the Congregation decreed: "The standard of living of our houses should not be higher than that of a family of slender means whose providers must work hard for its support" (Decree 12, n. 7). Jesuits have been grappling with the implications of these regulations to the present day.

It is not easy to live in the tension presented by Jesuit poverty. Yet it has been done, sometimes heroically. At the Thirty-second General Congregation Pedro Arrupe, the general superior, spoke of the consequences to the Society and to individual Jesuits if the Congregation voted for Decree Four on the faith that does justice. Not only might the Society alienate some of our influential alumni and alumnae and benefactors, but also individual Jesuits would be put at risk of their lives. In the event he was proved right. As Jesuits began to speak out for justice, they did indeed alienate some of their wealthy and influential friends. In just the last thirty years, over forty Jesuits have been murdered for their pursuit of justice for the poor. El Salvador provides notable examples. In 1977 Rutilio Grande, S.J. was killed on his way to say Mass, a murder that seems to have been the catalyst for the conversion of Archbishop Oscar Romero, his friend, to champion the cause of the poor of that country. At the same time, the Jesuits of the University of Central America (UCA) in El Salvador began to teach and do research from the side of the poor. Powerful and wealthy families turned away from them. In 1990 an army unit savagely murdered six Jesuit professors at UCA and their housekeeper and her daughter. Jesuits have paid a price for their commitment to the faith that does justice. No Jesuit, to our knowledge, has said that the Society should move back from that commitment because of the dangers. In fact, Jesuit volunteers took the places of these six Jesuits almost immediately after their murder. The latest General Congregation, the Thirty-fourth, has reconfirmed the commitment of the Thirty-second.

9. "A Unique Love": Creative Tensions in the Practice of Chastity

hat pertains to the vow of chastity requires no interpretation, since it is evident how perfectly it should be preserved, by endeavoring to imitate therein the purity of the angels in cleanness of body and mind. Therefore, with this presupposed, we shall now treat of holy obedience" (*Constitutions,* 547). This abrupt dispatch of a vow that has troubled many a Jesuit, at least in modern times, has inspired a good deal of humorous banter. Even when one factors in the notion that angels are mentioned because in the Bible they are depicted as God's messengers, whose only purpose is to help souls and who do not abuse the intimacy they have with those to whom they are sent, these words strike modern readers as rather unhelpful on how to live out the vow of chastity. In fact, recent General Congregations have found it appropriate to discourse on this vow at some length. To understand Jesuit spirituality it will be necessary to say something about how Jesuits try to live out this vow.

Prior to his conversion Ignatius seems to have been sexually active. In his memoirs he recounts a vision of Mary holding the child Jesus that gave him "a very extraordinary consolation. He was left so sickened at his whole past life, and especially at matters of the flesh, that it seemed to him that there had been removed from his soul all the likenesses that he had previously painted in it. Thus, from that hour until August 1553, when this is being written, he never again had even the slightest complicity in matters of the flesh" (*Personal Writings,* p. 16). We note that Ignatius does not say that he was freed of sexual desires, only that he had not succumbed to them. Moreover, this grace did not lead him to shun women. Throughout his life he maintained close relations with women. He gave spiritual direction to women as well as to men. Some women were benefactors who sustained and housed him in his pilgrim years and with whom he corresponded relatively frequently after he became general superior. And some women were close friends, as his letters to them testify. Whatever one makes of the words of the *Constitutions,* it is clear that for Ignatius the practice of the vow of chastity did not mean the cessation of sexual attraction nor require a physical distancing from women.

Earlier we noted one of the polarities described by John O'Malley: Jesuits had the cultural prejudices of their time with regard to women, but ministered to women in the same way as they ministered to men. O'Malley notes that women even more than men availed themselves of Jesuits for the confession of their sins. This ministry could get them into trouble, as happened in Venice and other places. In 1551 at Venice one of the Jesuits' friends tried to prevail on the superior of the Jesuits to forbid his men from hearing so many women's confessions because of the danger to the Jesuits' reputations. The rector refused on the grounds that it was part of their vocation. He referred the matter to Ignatius, who agreed with his decision. In time Jesuits did become concerned about their reputation and more cautious. Nonetheless, Jesuits in Rome, as late as 1561, were hearing confessions of sick women in their homes and continued to hear at least as many confessions of women as of men in their churches. Jesuit ministry brought them into situations that could give a wrong impression.

The early Jesuits did not live in fixed houses very often; they were on the road and had to take shelter wherever they could. This meant the use of inns, which often had an unsavory reputation, and of the homes of wealthy men and women. If they were to live the vow of chastity integrally, they had to do so from an inner core and conviction without many external helps. Cloister, for example, was not part of their early experience; they did not have houses to which lay men and women were forbidden entrance. Moreover, the kind of ministry in which they engaged brought them into close contact with women and men. They talked the language of the heart when they gave spiritual direction and counsel in confession.

There is no such thing as a spiritual conversation that remains only on the "spiritual plane."

When a person tells another about his or her prayer experiences or sins or sinful tendencies, he or she is engaging in a conversation of great intimacy. Such intimacy can evoke in both people feelings associated with close friendship and sexual attraction. Modern psychology has taught us that such intimate conversations, as in counseling or psychotherapy, also evoke feelings and emotions associated with important people in one's past. Those who seek counsel can, for example, project onto the counselor feelings associated with their parents or with other important authority figures. They may believe that their counselor is secretly in love with them or negatively judges them without any basis in reality. In psychoanalytic practice such reactions are called "transference." But counselors are also taught that their own past may be triggered by their clients. They may react negatively to some clients because they remind them of past figures who treated them badly; they may be erotically or sexually attracted to clients who remind them of loved ones in their past. Such reactions are called "countertransference." Jesuits who engage in this ministry need to know themselves quite well and also to be open with someone like a supervisor or spiritual director about their reactions.

The early Jesuits, and Jesuits after them who engaged in the ministry of spiritual conversation, must have experienced both "transference" and "countertransference" reactions, even if they did not know how to name them as such. Ignatius himself exerted a powerful attraction not only on women but also on men. Some of this attraction had to have been erotic, even if never acknowledged as such. The Jesuit psychoanalyst, William Meissner, remarks on Ignatius' attachment to his sister-in-law, Magdalena, who tended him during his recovery from his wounds. Ignatius, now the general superior, told one of his novices that a picture of the Virgin Mary in his prayer book so reminded him of Magdalena's beauty that he had to cover it in order that his intense affection for her might not be aroused. In spite of such powerful emotions and in spite of cautions about their reputations raised by their friends, neither Ignatius nor the early companions avoided the ministry of intimate conversation that both the giving of the Exercises and the hearing of confessions entailed. Nor did they avoid close friendships with men and women who were not fellow Jesuits. Jesuits are asked to live creatively in the tension of being faithful to their publicly-professed celibate chastity while engaging in ministries that easily evoke emotional and erotic impulses.

How do they manage to live their lives with integrity? First, as novices and then as tertians every Jesuit makes the full *Spiritual Exercises,* during which he finds himself called to be a companion of Jesus and to live as a celibate as Jesus did. The love of Jesus and the desire to be like him in all things motivate Jesuit chastity. This conviction that one is personally called by Jesus to celibate chastity for the sake of ministry and for the freedom to serve others is the heart of the matter. Second, Jesuits have a long and demanding formation in which they are expected to be open not only with their spiritual director but also with their superiors. When novices make the *Spiritual Exercises,* they learn how to talk about matters of the heart with their novice director. In the *Constitutions* Ignatius notes that the novice director should be a man whom the novices can love and trust, and adds that the novices

> should be advised, too, that they ought not to keep secret any temptation which they do not tell to him or to their confessor or to the superior, being happy to have their entire soul completely open to him. Moreover, they will tell him not only their defects but also their penances or mortifications, or their devotions and all their virtues, with a pure desire to be directed if in anything they have gone astray, and not wishing to be guided by their own judgment unless it is in agreement with the opinion of him whom they have in place of Christ our Lord. [263]

From the very beginning of their long formation Jesuits are urged to learn the importance of being open and honest with their spiritual directors and their superiors.

Later in the *Constitutions* Ignatius writes of all Jesuits: "Thus in everything they should proceed in a spirit of charity, keeping nothing exterior or interior hidden from the superiors and desiring them to be informed about everything, so that the superiors may be the better able to direct them in everything along the path of salvation and perfection" [551]. As we noted earlier, this openness in the account of conscience aims to help the superior in his decisions about the apostolic placement of his men. If he knows them intimately, it is more likely that he will assign them to work that is within their capacities, including their capacity to engage in the intimate ministry of spiritual conversation with real profit to others and without breaking professional boundaries, to use modern terminology. In addition, the Jesuit himself learns that being open and honest with other Jesuits is the best way to engage in ministry with integrity.

This is the ideal. Reality, of course, does not always match it. The ideal can be missed if the tensions involved in living the vow of chastity integrally are avoided. The cultural climate of a good part of the nineteenth and twentieth centuries focused on the dangers of any close encounter with the opposite sex and kept many Jesuits fearful of engaging in intimate spiritual conversations with others, except in very circumscribed circumstances. As the Society grew in numbers, it became more and more difficult for superiors to have an intimate knowledge of their men. We have already noted the difficulty of anything like an open and honest account of conscience during most of the past century because of the number of men under a provincial superior's care. Spiritual direction most often consisted of the confession of sins and the discussion of problems, not of a conversation about the movements of one's heart. Because of numbers, too, the Society, like most religious congregations, began to rely on regimentation and order more than on the interior spirit to maintain religious discipline. Even close relationships between Jesuits were discouraged as we noted in chapter 5.

In this climate fear of emotional closeness was engendered, and Jesuits did not learn how to live with the creative tension involved in the integral living of the vow of chastity while fully engaged in the world. This climate could and did produce men who seemed without emotional ties to anyone. The caricature, "They meet without affection and part without regret" had some validity. Some Jesuits seemed to live completely by logic and rule.

When Pope John XXIII threw open the windows of the church to the modern world at the Second Vatican Council, many Jesuits, indeed many religious, were not prepared for the emotional

73

upheavals that often accompanied the new freedoms. The Council coincided, at least in the United States, with the sexual revolution in ways of thinking about, acting on and portraying sexual activity. In this changed cultural climate it is no exaggeration to say that many Jesuits had to go through the throes of a delayed adolescence in order to arrive at a mature living out of the vow of chastity. After all, the majority had entered the Jesuits as adolescents and had grown up in a cloistered, all-male environment that was rather strongly regimented. Erik Erikson speaks of a moratorium in development during which, it seems, a young person is waiting for something to happen before moving on to the next stage of his psychological life. For those Jesuits who were in their thirties and early forties at the time of the Second Vatican Council, the period from their entrance until this time was like such a moratorium. Many had not negotiated the developmental crises that lead to psychological adulthood. In the turmoil of those heady years many decided that they could not live happily and productively as celibates and left the Society and married. Others stayed, but often not without inner struggle as they discovered how difficult it is to live the Jesuit vocation integrally.

During the period immediately after the Second Vatican Council, Father Arrupe, the general superior, felt compelled to write to all major superiors exhorting them to make sure that Jesuits realized that the "third way" of understanding the vow of chastity was unacceptable. According to this "third way," the vow of chastity meant that one did not marry, but it did not preclude sexual activity in a loving relationship. That Father Arrupe wrote the letter is an indication that some Jesuits were advocating this way, or questioning whether it might be compatible with the vow of chastity. There have been instances, we have to admit, when some Jesuits have violated their vow of chastity and seemed not to realize that their activity was unacceptable. General Congregations 31 and 32, and the *Complementary Norms* to the *Constitutions* approved by the most recent General Congregation 34, have found it necessary to address Jesuit chastity at some length with the aim of restoring or shoring up the creative tension that must be at the heart of any Jesuit's living of the vow. We can see how different our culture is

74

from that of Ignatius by the following words from the *Complementary Norms* that introduce the topic of chastity.

> By the vow of chastity, we devote ourselves to the Lord and to his service in such a unique love that it excludes marriage and any other exclusive human relationship, as well as the genital expression and gratification of sexuality. Thus the vow entails the obligation of complete continence in celibacy for the sake of the kingdom of heaven. Following the evangelical counsel of chastity, we aspire to deepen our familiarity with God, our configuration to Christ, our companionship with our brother Jesuits, our service to our neighbors whoever they may be; and at the same time we aspire to grow in our personal maturity and capacity to love. (144)

Clearly the Society has had to make explicit what the vow entails in this different cultural climate.

The recovery of the account of conscience and of a spiritual direction that requires openness about one's experience has been a great help in the restoration of the creative tension. Jesuits have once again learned the value of complete openness and honesty with superiors and with spiritual directors with the result that they have been able to appropriate the demands of living chastely, while being actively engaged in apostolic work that requires cooperation and friendship with male and female colleagues and close relationships with those to whom they minister. The recovery of an authentic Jesuit spirituality of creative tensions came at a providential moment in our history.

The question of sexual orientation has loomed large in the living of Jesuit chastity during recent years, especially in the United States and parts of Europe. Most people who have thought of the matter would probably agree that there have always been men and women in religious congregations whose sexual attractions were predominantly to those of their own sex. But this was never acknowledged. It was presumed that everyone who entered religious life was heterosexual in orientation. In a formation community that was segregated from the opposite sex, it was known that young men or young women might be attracted to one or other of their coreligious, but this was considered an aberration that would fade after they moved on from formation to apostolic work in the wider world. In Jesuit novitiates, as we have mentioned, novices were cautioned against "particular friendships" and forbidden to touch one another even in games. But the presumption was that all the men were heterosexual in orientation. As a result those who were aware that their attractions were toward the same sex kept this secret for the most part, and they often presumed that they were aberrant and even sinful because of their orientation. One can get a sense of how Jesuits whose orientation was homosexual felt about their status in the Society from the following incident. During an address at a province assembly a provincial noted that the Society of Jesus consisted of men who were conservative and liberal, Republican, Democrat and Independent, heterosexual and homosexual in orientation, and that all of us must learn how to live together as brothers and to love one another. After the talk a number of men whose orientation was homosexual approached the provincial to thank him and to say that it was the first time that any Jesuit in authority had acknowledged that they were part of the Society.

In the past twenty or thirty years there has been another sexual revolution, namely the growing gay and lesbian movement to overcome some of the prejudices and injustices aimed at gays and lesbians. Religious congregations have not been immune from the effects of this movement. Jesuits who are homosexual in orientation have grown increasingly unwilling to hide from their superiors and their fellow religious who they are. In addition, as some recent reports about seminaries and religious houses have indicated, the proportion of homosexual men in seminaries and religious congregations seems to be higher than in the population at large. Jesuit communities have also had to come to terms with these realities. They have had to learn to trust one another as men who want to and are trying to live integrally with the creative tension that the Jesuit vow of chastity entails regardless of sexual orientation. It has not always been easy to come to this level of trust. But it has happened and is happening as we write these pages, and the Society of Jesus is the richer and more effective in its apostolic activity as a result.

10. Conclusion: Finding God in All Things

hroughout this short work on Jesuit spirituality we have maintained that this spirituality cannot be understood without grasping the creative tensions that fuel the energies of its adherents. At the heart of these creative tensions, however, is a reality: namely, the faith-based experience that our triune God, who transcends everything created is, nonetheless, actively working in this world to bring about God's rule or project and wants men and women to cooperate in this project. God, the transcendent and immanent one, is the source of the tensions inherent in Jesuit spirituality. The present general superior, Peter-Hans Kolvenbach, has written:

> Probably, Ignatius was the first person in the history of Christian spirituality to perceive the Trinity as God at work—as the God who continues to work, always filling up the universe and actively awakening the divine life in all things for the salvation of humanity. If the inspired monk contemplates, the inspired Ignatius works—adhering with all his heart to the designs of the Trinity, offering himself to act in synergy with the Trinity so that his work is for the Trinity's glory. In that way, the Trinitarian attraction in Ignatius' devotion tends to embrace the whole of humankind. His devotion seeks only God, not, however, only for himself, but rather for all his brothers and sisters. Thus might all created things, not evil in themselves but often averted by humankind from their source and origin, return with humanity to true meaning in God. (*The Road from La Storta*, 23–24)

Jesuits, taking their cue from Ignatius, find the transcendent triune God always at work in the world and try, with the help of God, to work together with God. Thus, when they are true to their spirituality, they try to find God in all things, in their prayer, in their apostolic activity, even in their play, while, at the same time, trying to keep in mind that God is always greater than any of these. A story is told of St. John Berchmans, a Jesuit scholastic who died before he could be ordained. Once, while playing billiards, he was asked what he would do if he were to find out that he would die in a few minutes. He is said to have replied: "I would go on playing billiards." An apt illustration of how someone imbued with Jesuit spirituality might find God in all things.

Kolvenbach's reference to God at work recalls the "Contemplation for attaining love," the final exercise of the *Spiritual Exercises*, considered its climax or capstone. In that exercise Ignatius asks the person to contemplate four points: how much God has done for me, how God dwells in the whole of creation and in me, how God works and labors on my behalf, how all good gifts descend from on high. The first and third points of the "Contemplation" are especially relevant to Kolvenbach's thesis:

> Point 1—This is to bring to memory the benefits received—creation, redemption, and particular gifts—pondering with great affection how much God Our Lord has done for me, and how much He has given me of what He has; and further, how according to His divine plan, it is the Lord's wish, as far as He is able, to give me Himself.... [234]

> Point 3—To consider how God works and labors on my behalf in all created things on the face of the earth, i.e., 'He behaves in the same way as a person at work,' as in the heavens, elements, plants, fruits, cattle, etc. He gives being, conserves life, grants growth and feeling, etc.... [236]

Those who engage in this exercise want to be able to *contemplate* how God gives himself and how God works in all things. That is, they want to experience God as continually giving and as always working at all times and in all things. The Jesuit who has made this exercise at least twice in his life in the Society, as the climax of the thirty-day *Spiritual Exercises,* tries to live in this world as one who is thus gifted and who is called to work in tune with the God who thus works. Hence the importance of the examen of conscience which he is asked to make at least twice a day.

We look upon the examen of conscience as analogous to the period of reflection suggested by Ignatius after each exercise in the *Spiritual Exercises*. During the *Exercises* one reflects on the prayer exercise just completed to see how it went, to notice consolations and desolations, to discern what movements were of God, which not. In this way one becomes attuned to how God is leading and also how one strays from God's direction. When a Jesuit makes the examen of conscience, for example, around noon of a particular day, he considers the time from waking as similar to a time of prayer in the *Exercises*. During this time God, he believes, has been active in his life because God is always active in this world. Now he wonders whether he experienced God's activity, that is, whether, like the disciples on the road to Emmaus, his heart was burning without his being fully aware of it, and whether he was in tune with God's activity or not. By engaging in this kind of reflection over time he hopes to become more of a contemplative in action, namely, one who quite literally finds God in all things, in prayer, in work, in recreation.

Jesuits want to be men who live happily and creatively with the tensions inherent in their spirituality. They see themselves as called to be companions of Jesus just as the apostles were called. The Thirty-second General Congregation asked:

> What is it to be a Jesuit? It is to know that one is a sinner, yet called to be a companion of Jesus as Ignatius was: Ignatius, who begged the Blessed Virgin to "place him with her Son," and who then saw the Father himself ask Jesus, carrying his Cross, to take this pilgrim into his company.
>
> What is it to be a companion of Jesus today? It is to engage, under the standard of the cross, in the crucial struggle of our time: the struggle for faith and that struggle for justice which it includes. (Decree 2, "Jesuits Today: A response of the 32nd General Congregation to requests for a description of Jesuit identity in our time")

Jesuits want to be true to this definition. Because they believe, and in that belief experience—that the triune God working in the world wants them to cooperate in that work—they find themselves caught up in the tensions we have outlined in this book. They try to work as if everything depended on God, but they also use all their talent, as well as whatever means seem adapted to attain their aims. To some they look like dreamers who waste their talent and efforts on a losing cause. To others they look like the neo-pagans with whom they often live and work. To others they seem so threatening that they become the enemy to be attacked and even killed. When they live within the creative tensions of their spirituality, they are as problematic as Jesus, their Lord, who has called them to be his companions.

BIBLIOGRAPHY

WORKS CITED

Clancy, S.J., Thomas H., "St. Ignatius as Fund-Raiser," *Studies in the Spirituality of Jesuits,* 25/1, January, 1993.

Cordara, S.J., Giulio Cesare, *On the Suppression of the Society of Jesus: A Contemporary Account,* translated by John P. Murphy, S.J. Chicago: Loyola Press, 1999.

Documents of the 31st and 32nd General Congregations of the Society of Jesus. St. Louis: Institute of Jesuit Sources, 1977.

Kolvenbach, S.J. Peter-Hans, *The Road from La Storta.* St. Louis: Institute of Jesuit Sources, 2000.

Meissner, S.J., M.D., William W. *Ignatius of Loyola: The Psychology of a Saint.* New Haven and London: Yale University Press, 1992.

O'Malley, S.J., John, *The First Jesuits.* Cambridge, Mass. and London: Harvard University Press, 1993.

Ravier, S.J., André, *Ignatius of Loyola and the Founding of the Society of Jesus,* translated by Maura Daly, Joan Daly and Carson Daly. San Francisco: Ignatius Press, 1987.

Saint Ignatius of Loyola, *Personal Writings,* translated with introductions and notes by Joseph A. Munitiz and Philip Endean. London and New York: Penguin, 1996. (Contains "Reminiscences," "Spiritual Diary," "Select Letters," and the *Spiritual Exercises* with introductions and notes.)

The Constitutions of the Society of Jesus and their Complementary Norms, General Editor, John W. Padberg. St. Louis: Institute of Jesuit Sources, 1996.

Barry, S.J., William A., *Finding God in All Things: A Companion to the Spiritual Exercises of St. Ignatius.* Notre Dame, Ind.: Ave Maria Press, 1991. (Based on lectures given during the Ignatian year, each chapter takes up a section of the *Exercises.*)

————, *What Do I Want in Prayer?* New York/Mahwah: Paulist Press, 1994. (This book is made for someone who wants to make the *Spiritual Exercises* in daily life. It can be taken to work or anyplace and used when one has the time.)

Broderick, S.J., James, *The Origin of the Jesuits.* Second Edition. Chicago: Loyola Press, 2000. (A well-written, passionate history of the founding of the Jesuits first published in 1940 by the distinguished English Jesuit historian.)

————, *The Progress of the Jesuits (1556-1579).* Chicago: Loyola Press, 1986. (A sequel to the earlier volume published originally in 1946.)

Byron, S.J., William J., *Jesuit Saturdays: Sharing the Ignatian Spirit with Lay Colleagues and Friends.* Chicago: Loyola Press, 2000. (A useful introduction to Ignatian spirituality.)

Caraman, S.J., Philip, *Ignatius Loyola: A Biography of the Founder of the Jesuits.* San Francisco: Harper & Row, 1990. (A well-written biography by another English Jesuit.)

Echaniz, S.J., Ignacio, *Passion and Glory: A Flesh-and-Blood History of the Society of Jesus.* Chicago: Loyola Press, 2000. (Four volumes that tell the stories of more than 150 Jesuits from the beginning to the present.)

Letson, Douglas and Michael Higgins, *The Jesuit Mystique.* Chicago: Loyola Press, 1995. (Two lay scholars present the Society of Jesus in its history and its present, culling the results of interviews of over 100 Jesuits and men and women who are intimately connected with Jesuits.)

Lonsdale, David, *Eyes to See, Ears to Hear: An Introduction of Ignatian Spirituality.* Second edition, revised and expanded. New York: Orbis, 2000. (An insightful introduction by a former Jesuit of the English province.)

Martin, S.J., James, *In Good Company: The Fast Tack from the Corporate World to Poverty, Chastity and Obedience.* Franklin, Wis.: Sheed & Ward, 2000. (An engaging and entertaining book by a young Jesuit describing his vocation and his first years in the Society of Jesus.)

O'Malley, S.J., William J., *The Fifth Week.* Second Edition. Afterword by James Martin, S.J. Chicago: Loyola Press, 2001. (A lively, well-written book explaining to prospective candidates the life of Jesuits after the "four weeks" of the *Spiritual Exercises.*)

Silf, Margaret, *Inner Compass: An Invitation to Ignatian Spirituality.* Chicago: Loyola Press, 1999. (A British laywoman presents Ignatian spirituality in a lively, imaginative style.)

Other Robert J. Wicks Spirituality Selections

Simply SoulStirring by Francis Dorff, O. Praem.
Transforming Fire by Kathleen Fischer
Living the Hospitality of God by Lucien Richard, O.M.I.
Seeking Spiritual Growth through the Bible
by Wilfrid J. Harrington, O.P.